D0462813

THE BECOMERS

OTHER BOOKS BY KEITH MILLER

The Taste of New Wine

A Second Touch

Habitation of Dragons

KEITH MILLER

THE BECOMERS

Word Books, Publisher

Waco, Texas

Library of Congress Catalog Card number: 72-96363

Printed in the United States of America

To

Robert Dentan, Elton Trueblood, and Earl Koile,
the teachers who first took me with
them into the lands of the Hebrews, the
philosophers, and the caring humanistic
psychologists.

And to

Earle and Mabel Miller
who loved me and told me never to be
afraid to look for the truth.

Contents

Acknowledgments

I am grateful to the authors and publishers whose words are cited for permission to quote from their works. And I am deeply indebted to those teachers, students, authors, and friends whose ideas have slipped unconsciously into my bloodstream and may have surfaced here as my own. I have been as careful as possible to give credit, but so many of you have helped me that I could never acknowledge your influence.

All of the biblical quotations are from the Revised Standard Version of 1952 unless otherwise identified.

The following friends read all or part of this book in manuscript form: John Glancy, Brooks Goldsmith, Tiny Hawn, Chuck and Carolyn Huffman, Vester Hughes, Ann Hutchinson, Lois Knox, Bob Parker, and Gene Warr. I am particularly grateful to John Knox, Patricia Prewitt, and Clif Williams for help with the biblical and psychological materials. Their thoughtful suggestions and criticisms were valuable in helping me to see what I was doing and saying. But since I did not follow all their suggestions, I cannot blame anyone but myself for the mistakes you may find.

Floyd Thatcher as usual went far beyond the call of duty as editor, as did his editorial associates at Word. And I want to thank Dennis Hill for his help with the illustrations and cover designs for this book and my last book, *Habitation of Dragons*.

Emma Ward, Frances Engle, and Mavis Knox typed and encouraged when I was ready to forget the whole thing. My colleagues and students at the Earlham School of Religion last year gave me the affirmation and freedom to use some of the material and approach suggested in this book in teaching seminary classes in communication and counseling.

And my wife, Mary-Allen, was prophet, lover, speller, and grammarian during the "desert period" near the end of the book.

For the Reader:

Fifteen years ago many denominational officials and members of seminary communities were shaking their heads in mild surprise and distaste at the beginning of what looked like an embarrassing outbreak of pietistic "conversions" in the church. These leaders remembered the psychological rigidity and exclusiveness of many nineteenth-century pietists who had "arrived" through conversion experiences. The church's scholars had rebelled against the tight fundamentalism which seemed to motivate the behavior of those earlier Christian converts. The general consensus (and hope) in the church hierarchies seemed to be that this time the blossoming "renewal" would blow over after a brief emotional binge.

But it has not blown over. And what few people noticed at first is that a core strand of the contemporary renewal movement produces a very different kind of person. The new convert sees the Christian life and process of growth very differently from his nineteenth-century counterpart. Instead of a doctrinaire and vertical exclusiveness with God, the new Christian is moving toward deeper and more honest personal relationships with people in the world—as well as with God. But by using personal honesty and vulnerability as a style of communication, the convert is often repugnant and confusing to the objectively oriented pastor or seminary professor.

Besides having a deeper relatedness with people, these new Christians are seeing that conversion is only a "beginning" and not an "arrival." The convert has just been freed to *start* actualizing the gifts and potentialities which have always been inherent in his life. He thinks of himself as a "becomer" in process. Some are beginning to find their own creativity and freedom. They are discovering richness and love in each other's lives as they share their struggles. Many are getting in touch with their own true feelings and are learning to give away their new life-style in Christ to other people.

Another mark of the "becomers" is a rebelliousness at treating Christianity as a safe abstraction. Christian growth has to do with risking one's psychological and material securities in the world for others, and thus for God. At its best, this bent toward "concrete" living is not anti-intellectual at all. Not only are such areas as biblical studies and history emphasized, but the new Christian has had to take the discoveries of modern psychology very seriously. He has found that his unconscious life is filled with both good and bad things which he has unknowingly repressed and which cripple his relationships to God, to other people, and to the self he might become. He has discovered that he is motivated by needs about which he knows very little. From the outside these "becoming" Christians often remind me of the liberated people described by the human potential movement in psychology . . . but with an inner difference.

Those of us who are a part of this strange group of unfolding lives have talked and talked—and often alienated people for miles around by our enthusiasm. Our friends and families either think we're crazy, or join us. Our ministers or bishops are either thrilled or appalled to hear us speak so personally about God and about conversion. They want to know what we mean by the terms we use. So far this has been a real problem, since many of us have been stuck with the word symbols of nineteenth-century piety, which do not accurately describe the experience of "becoming" at all.

And so some serious questions have been raised concerning our methods of communicating the gospel, our beliefs about personality development, and our ideas concerning growth in the Christian life. This book looks at several of these questions. They were raised originally in small groups of becomers. The laymen and pastors in these groups were struggling. They were trying to live and communicate their new faith in a world which could not hear their experience because of their archaic language. Although the questions came from several groups of which I have been a member over the past fifteen years, for the sake of simplicity, I will refer to "our group" or "our strugglers' group" throughout the book as if there had been only one.

The four questions around which the book is written are:

1. Why the "personal" stance in communicating the gospel?
2. What's inside, behind our masks?
3. What happens in conversion?
4. What about Christian growth?

And there is an Epilogue concerning a Christian's attitudes toward the social and political aspects of the world.

I am writing to those of you who are wrestling with these questions as a part of your own lives and also to those who are trying to communicate the gospel to other people. I have searched everywhere for words and symbols to describe that which is taking place in my own life and throughout the church. It is out of this struggle to find and develop communication models for becomers that this book is written.

A few of the ideas developed in the first chapters were mentioned briefly in earlier books or articles as the notion of becoming was first developing in my experience.

The second section, particularly chapters 8 through 13, constitutes a definite change of pace and tone from the rest of the book. These chapters deal with psychological concepts and are more abstract than the material either before or after them.

KEITH MILLER
Port Aransas, Texas

Question I

Why the "Personal" Stance
in Communicating the Gospel?

One

Beginning with a Failure

IT was late, time to go home, and I was bone tired. I had tried everything I knew to get that group of fourteen men and women to communicate personally with each other. But I'd failed . . . again.

We had wanted something significant to happen to and through the people in our church. Both ministers, one of whom was in this group, had preached about "renewal" from the pulpit. I had talked about it for over a year in the large adult class. Finally we had started an experimental small group. The purpose of the group was to learn how to become God's open loving people in our city. We had decided that the first step was to try to learn to communicate with each other at more than a surface level.

Coming into the first meeting we had felt the excitement of being part of a new experiment. The noise level was high before the meeting started, and there was a lot of

17

nervous laughter. At first we tried to get to know each other by introducing ourselves. We wanted to be real. But our introductions and responses were so careful and superficial that we were still virtually strangers when the introductions were finished. I remember looking around the group in a kind of inner amazement as I realized that some of us had been attending the same church for years and knew almost nothing about each other's personal feelings concerning anything which was truly important to us.

"And," I thought, "we still don't."

After more sparring, I suggested that we try something different. We were to take turns talking. Each of us would take six minutes. During the first five minutes we had to relate those things which popped into our minds out of our past which we thought might have contributed to making us what we are today. If anyone failed to take the full five minutes, the group members could fill in the time by asking any personal question which occurred to them. During the sixth minute each person was to relate the happiest experience he could recall. One man was designated "timer," and it was his job to interrupt on the second to announce the time.

As we started, there was more nervous laughter. The first person said her happiest experience was her wedding. Next came her husband, and he had no choice but to agree. We were a group made up primarily of couples. And after that beginning most people related basically positive things about their marriages. We all knew that we were somehow faking it with each other and that our newest hope for an experience of Christian community was a miserable failure.

As we were about to end the meeting, one woman

interrupted, "Wait a minute. I haven't said anything."
And she was right. This woman had been so quiet I had
forgotten she was there. We all looked at her. She was a
very slender woman about thirty years old. Painfully uneasy, she seemed to be holding her plain wool suit together
at the throat. After looking at me a few seconds, evidently
deciding whether or not to say it, she began.

"I've been sitting here feeling awful. I don't have anything in common with you," and she gestured toward us
all. "You talk about happy marriages, and ours has been
touch-and-go at best—and often *terrible*. And only
through a lot of good marriage counseling have we come
up with a marriage where we are even beginning to find
any real communication and love. You speak of happy
childhoods. Mine was miserable. My first memory [we
had asked about first memories] is of my mother's red
face screaming at my father to 'get out of our lives and
stay out!' He left and never came back. I wasn't quite
three years old, but I remember being afraid and lonely
that night. And I've been afraid and lonely every night
since.

"As for the happiest moment in my life. I remember
one Christmas Eve when my younger sister and I were
still little girls. We didn't expect anything much for
Christmas because we were very poor after my father left.
But that night we had been out and came home late. It
was miserably cold and had just gotten dark. The door
was locked, and we had to climb through a window from
the front porch. I pushed back the shade. And there, in
the corner of the living room, was a Christmas tree with
only a few scraggly lights on it—the only lights in the
room. I remember, as I crawled in the window, seeing
under the tree in the soft glow of those lights, two doll

bassinets, each with a live-skin dolly in it, and a pink coverlet. We couldn't imagine where my mother had gotten the money for such presents . . ."

The young woman had become soft and different . . . like a child. She stopped talking, remembering. And we were very still. Then she looked at us and raised her eyebrows, "And that was the happiest moment in my life."

"But you know," and she shook her head sadly, "I realize that I don't belong in this group. I didn't finish high school, and you're all college graduates. I've never known *any* real acceptance, and you're all successful socially."

She paused, looked down, and said simply, "I guess I just want what you already have."

We sat there, stunned by the reality which had drawn us irresistibly toward this thin, totally unprotected young woman. And I realized that it was *we* who needed what *she* had—the ability to be personal and honest in a vulnerable way. As I looked around at the group, I knew that somehow, because this theologically unsophisticated young woman had turned loose of her silence and her pride and reached out in total honesty, it was at last safe for us to start becoming one in Jesus Christ.

A change came over the group right then. Some people confessed that they hadn't been totally honest about things being so perfect in their lives. And as we let down the unreal walls of our perfection, several very striking things began to happen that night and in the weeks and months which followed.

For one thing, the quality and clarity of the communication—of hearing and being heard—improved immensely. We didn't have to explain "what we meant" nearly as much after we spoke of our true feelings. And our prayers became specific and related to actual problems or changes for which we were thankful. Over the next year we got to know each other. And we began to learn how to give and receive help with our difficulties of believing and living. To try to understand our behavior we looked into psychology, along with the Scriptures. And with great release we found that a lot of the problems and tensions we thought had evil and spiritual causes were simply normal experiences of being human in a tense and over-stimulated generation. We began to have "breakthrough" moments of self-insight and freedom from the tyranny of long-past hates and fears.

As we looked at our faith, several people confessed that they were not very strongly motivated to be Christians. Some had secretly wondered if they needed a "conversion." Others had been through some kind of experience as a young person, but weren't sure if they were really converted. In short, we realized we didn't know what a genuine conversion experience should feel like. And finally, after deciding to commit our lives to the finding and doing of God's will, some of us began asking what it might mean to move into the awesome agony, loneliness, and dehumanization of social and political structures. As a result of being more open with each other, we were feeling more free and happy about life and more inclined to be loving. This was true even though some of us were going through very painful circumstances.

During the years since that group meeting, I have realized something of the power, the threat, and some of the dangers of communicating in an atmosphere of personal vulnerability. I now believe that although technique is involved, the primary condition for being an effective communicator of God's love and message is a *life-style*.

The communicator, it seems, must honestly feel that *he* is a struggling becomer himself and not an expert in living the Christian life—however much information about that life he may have.

This personal approach to communicating the faith is not in opposition to the social or political dimensions of Christianity. As a matter of fact, many who have gotten involved in social action ventures *without* understanding their own struggles and need to "become" have failed miserably and are bitter and cynical men and women.

The discussions in the rest of this book will be dealing with questions about the life-style and approach to the Christian faith being experienced by becomers in a new awakening. Actually I believe what is happening in the church is part of a larger historical experience. We seem to be in the midst of a revolution in approaches to communication.

Two

A Revolution
in Communication

W E were standing in front of a computer in the room next to the regional computer bank in a large state university. For a group of graduate students in psychology we were (I thought) strangely quiet. The young lady leading us through the center said, "Here's a simple model. You can talk to it—through that typewriter. Ask it anything you want to." Finally one student sat down and typed out "Howdy—hello!" In less time than it takes to write this, the machine began to type back, "Hello there, welcome to the University of Texas!" When it stopped, the young man sat there a few seconds, then turned to us and said rather wistfully, "That's the warmest thing that's been said to me around here in three years." And although we laughed, several of us felt the truth behind what he was saying. The human kindness which many of the professors no longer have time for is having to be built into machines to motivate the struggling students.

To talk about the speed of change in the area of communication is to rehash that which is being said all around us. But the number of sales pitches each of us receives every day from the mass media is almost unbelievable. We find ourselves wading in a thick swamp of choices, most of which we did not instigate. For instance, Alvin Toffler (1971) in *Future Shock* indicated that we can have a million different combinations of styles and accessories to choose from in buying a Mustang automobile.

We are the object of so much communication that many of us have an increasing need to push it *all* away and get some emotional space. But it keeps coming. The sounds of the telephone, radio, TV, or Muzak surround us. It seems to be snowing flurries of magazines, books, letters, and direct-mail pieces. I have a stack of unread books and magazines on the table beside me which have already been screened from a much larger stack. Some of these I *need* to read—but I cannot find time.

"The flesh is crying out" from inside, *Stop it! Leave me alone!* And we are scratching out emotional caves in which to hide from the din of words and images which chase us through our days and nights. We hide in alcohol, drugs, sexual overstimulation, travel, compulsive working, sterile religious meetings, and nervous breakdowns. Toffler (1971, p. 326) has given our reaction the name *future shock:* "We may define future shock as the distress, both physical and psychological, that arises from an overload of the human organism's physical adaptive systems and its decision-making processes. Put more simply, future shock is the human response to overstimulation."

We can no longer respond and integrate the "new thing" into our lives—even new information with life or death significance. Instead, we often watch with a sort of numb detachment as people and environments are injured or destroyed. One result of these bewildering developments has been that we have changed the way we listen.

What has happened? Evidently in order to avoid the barrage of noises aimed at us, we have developed a protective psychic screening device, a sort of grid or filter. This filter only lets verbal communication through which sounds as if it will *help us in our efforts to meet our own most pressing personal needs and accomplish our own goals.*

Since we would go insane listening to the content of every communication, the psychic filter automatically screens out messages which don't "sound like" our *approach to life.* For instance, let's say that I am driving along in my car and flip on the radio. If a breathy quivering voice comes on saying something like, *"Ya gotta believeeve in Jesus!"* I change the station automatically. At one level I realize that the speaker could have something new and perceptive to tell me about our Lord. But I shut him out because he does not have my "sound."

Each denominational group seems to have developed its own sounds—certain pat phrases, intonations or different names with which God is addressed in worship: "Our Father," "Father God," "O Lord," "Lord Jesus," "Jesus," "Our Heavenly Father," and so on. I have been speaking in different denominational churches for more than ten years. And if I could ask a dozen ministers whom I'd never met to lead a group of you in prayer, I'll bet I could tell in several instances the denomination in which they were trained. And when *your* man prayed, you would say "āmen"—unless of course your group is like ours and says "ahmen."

Somehow we are consciously or unconsciously trained to distrust people in other religious groups, *and we can recognize them and tune them out by their "sound."*

But even *within* denominations there are different "sounds." There is a "high church" formal sound, a "low church" evangelical sound, an "educated-philosophical" sound. And in all groups I've been exposed to there is a "ministerial" sound.

But all of these "sounds" are only outward symbols of whole different clusters of preconceived notions about what it means to be a Christian and live a Christian life. For years our different "sounds" have separated us in the Body of Christ. And unfortunately, our religious noises have turned off people outside the church who might have been interested in the truth about life contained in the gospel. The world in general has simply screened out our religious-sounding communication without hearing it because it does not sound like anything important in their lives.

The baffling part about this tragedy is that in *one's own group* the members aren't aware that they have a different sound because they cannot hear their own. Consequently, in our own churches we don't ordinarily realize how ridiculous we sound to the rest of the world.

Several years ago I was at a dinner where one of the most gifted Christian communicators of our time was speaking. He was talking about ways to set the ideas you want to communicate into the context of the audience's lives. When he came into a new community to speak, he always bought a local newspaper and read it through. If there had been a devastating tragedy in that town, the audience would be in a very different mood than if there were an all-city celebration coming up for the high-school state championship basketball team.

The speaker said that one Sunday he was to speak in Bloomington, Illinois. He arrived Saturday evening and bought a paper. It seems that there are two small towns or suburbs next to Bloomington—one called "Normal" and the other "Oblong." As the speaker was turning through the paper, he came to the society section, and his eyes were drawn to a headline: "Normal boy marries Oblong girl." He thought this was hilarious, cut it out, and read it from the pulpit the next morning. But no one laughed. The names of the towns were so much a part of their own local language that they couldn't see how funny they might sound to the rest of the world.

And I believe we in the church are in a similar position with regard to our communicating to people outside the Christian community. We do not realize how unreal our language and "in" expressions are. Because all of our sounds have one thing in common: *They are different from the sounds of everyday life!* And to the uninitiated they seem pious or phony. Very few couples I know fight or make love in King James English. The men and women with whom I counsel have problems, anxieties, and doubts which don't have a religious sound. And in my own life— when I scream silently at night in my aloneness and frustration—I do not do it in the language of the liturgy, or systematic theology.

A part of the current awakening in the church is that men and women are beginning to hear and speak about Christianity in the language and thought patterns of life—ordinary life. Professor of Old Testament James Wharton has said in summarizing the Bible story, "Real human thoughts, not religious thoughts, are the Christian ones." The sound of *Life!* And the exciting thing is that people respond to life—black people, white people, young people, old people, men and women, Southern people, and Northern. The gospel with the ring of life is getting into the arena of people's lives. And the spokesmen in this strange Christian reformation are men and women who have the sound of ordinary life even if they are theologically sophisticated.

But the sound of life only gets the Christian's message into the atmosphere of ordinary folk. The message still has to compete with all the other lifelike sounds before it can get *through* people's defensive filters into their *inner* lives. And since men and women only seem to let that information into their inner lives which pertains to *their own* most pressing needs and goals, how can Christians find out what these most pressing needs are?

Three

A Silent Cry

W HAT are the pressing inner needs which haunt us
and motivate us to keep listening for direction in the
midst of a hurricane of irrelevant words?

Each generation seems to experience at least one central
pervasive individual problem which colors every area of
life it touches. I have come to believe that many of the
more obvious *social* conflicts are often symptoms of deeper
common *personal* dilemmas—and not the other way
around. And great renewal in Christian societies has
taken place when persons or groups within the church
have begun to see the way in which the gospel speaks
specifically to that generation's central human problem—
as it is experienced by the common man.

In the early Middle Ages life for most people was crude
by our standards. Primitive comforts like the fireplace and
the transparent window glass were just being made available. Life was relatively dirty, short, and miserable. So the

church's message was concentrated on the beauty of heaven—clean, peaceful, eternal, and joyous. The art of the time often illustrated this message. And of course for those who rejected Christ or were unrepentant evildoers, there was a vivid and eternal hell—which only seemed to emphasize the attractiveness of heaven.

But this focus on the joys of heaven does not get through most people's communication filters today. In our home we have more clean and beautiful things than most of the extravagant visions of heaven from the ancient painters and poets. Here I can even control the temperature. Through telephone and television we can communicate with the entire world. In my own living room I can see fish mating at the bottom of the sea, men actually murdered, the earth from the moon . . . there are no longer any "foreign lands."

If this is true—that the fear of physical deprivation and early death are not the most gnawing personal problems for many people in affluent America—then how do we find *our* generation's special problem in the midst of the thousands of cries for help and attention all around us? It seems doubly important to try to recognize our most pressing existential problem since the change and cure of society depends on it. As Alfred North Whitehead (1955, p. 90) pointed out, civilized order "is transformed by its power of recognizing its imperfections."

We in the church have often been proud of preaching brilliant sermons about broad social issues. However, our audiences do not hear because they are in a silent death struggle with something *they* consider to be personally more immediate and threatening, though their problems may seem petty and selfish even to them.

But what are people gripped by now?

Through the skill and aggressiveness of modern advertising—particularly on television—we know more about each other's homes and personal habits than any previous generation has. Advertising has created an illusion of intimacy and joy that certainly rivals heaven (for those who buy the right products). I know something about what kind of cereal you eat, what you shave with, and what kind of clothes you wear in every room in your house. If I could talk to half a dozen of the women reading this book and find out your financial and social status, I could probably describe your underwear fairly accurately. I have no doubt seen it all on television or in the magazines.

But there are some difficulties with these highly touted Madison Avenue versions of intimacy and joy. They *aren't really intimate or joyful.* And yet we are told again and again that they are. And when we buy the "right" products and don't feel whole, we doubt ourselves. Consequently, there is a strong drive to appear neat, cool, and adequate in all circumstances regardless of how lonely or hopeless we feel. We learn from the most beautiful advertising models in the world how to hide feelings if they are unattractive or inadequate. And apparently those of us in my generation will buy anything that promises adequacy or will cover up our haunting sense of not being "enough."

There seems to be only one area in my life which the television camera has not penetrated with its fantasizing lens—and that is inside my mind, behind this facade of my face which I show to the rest of you. In here I am not the clever masculine performer I try to be when I am with you. In here I am often alone and uncertain about me and the future and about you and how you feel about me. And since almost all of us know how to *appear* to be happy and well adjusted from the time we are old enough to sit in front of the tube, any restless sense of incompleteness and loneliness I experience is even more poignant when I look at you. Possibly some may feel that this picture is overdrawn. But anyone who does personal counseling realizes how much agony is hidden underneath our facades. For behind our masks all is not rosy and untroubled.

In a recent discussion, psychiatrists Jean Rosenbaum, Natalie Shainers, and Antonio Wenkart agreed that poignant loneliness is the most dangerous and widespread illness in America today. They felt that loneliness had already reached epidemic proportions, and if it continued to spread, it would destroy the United States as a nation. Loneliness, they agreed, is now man's worst enemy. Since World War II, it has spread like a plague. "Chronic loneliness nowadays affects from 75 to 90 percent of all Americans," Dr. Rosenbaum said. The basic symptoms of loneliness she cited are a sense of despair at feeling unloved and a hidden fear of being unwanted. Lonely people live in a world of restless incompleteness and often do destructive things to get rid of their terrors. To keep our balance of sanity, we must have a sense of belonging to something important or to someone we value.

I think the deeply personal restless incompleteness from which loneliness often stems is the root of our generation's central human problem—which is *meaningless depersonalization.*

But strangely, the problem is almost worse for Christians. We are subtly trained that if *we* are really restless or lonely, it may be a reflection on the depth of our commitment. So we repress these feelings and are conscious only of a strange franticness, or even boredom, or lack of interest in Christianity—which also can produce guilt. Or, on the other hand, if we express our feelings of inadequacy and emptiness publicly, we are told that non-Christians might not want our faith—and so this kind of honesty in our communication would "hurt our witness for Christ." So of all our generation, we Christians are sometimes the most frustrated and lonely, with our solitary self-doubts, fears, and conflicts.

This restless, lonely, and sometimes frightening sense of unfulfillment spans all of the group divisions of our day. Young people feel it acutely and are reaching in all directions for the "personal." And their "new morality" has assured many of them at an early age that sex will not overcome this deeper need for worth and completeness. But old people feel empty and frantic too as they demand security and feel shunted aside by families and society. Men feel this impersonal emptiness and rush after sex, power, and acceptance. And in a new way women are demanding and getting the right to join the scramble on an equal basis. Rich people and poor people feel the creeping impersonalness in their inner lives. And the black (or anyone from the third world) is extremely serious in his attempts to end this depersonalization, which he often seems to think is uniquely his experience in our time. But it is *not,* even though the sense of separation is bound to be much worse for him because of his high visibility in a predominately white society in the western world.

No, we are all caught in the web of depersonalization.

Four

The Personal:
a Key to the Lonely Cell

IF it is true—that the underlying pressing problems within our lives stem from lonely, restless unfulfillment that can't be met by material comforts—then how do we begin to communicate *the gospel* in a way that can be heard through the filters of this restless overstimulated generation? The church's answer to loneliness has often been proximity: "fellowship," "involvement," "get with them," "help them," or "preach them the message." And our church communication strategies often follow these notions about conveying the Christian gospel. But somehow they are not working—even as some of these approaches appeared to work in the past. Real involvement which is personal can not, it seems, be programed. I can remember the carnage of dozens of Sunday afternoons in our home when my father announced to the family through gritted teeth, "We are going to do something *as a family today*—just to have *fun* together—does everyone *understand* that?" Fellowship could not be artificially manufactured in our family. And I don't believe it can be in our institutions.

No, if restless, lonely incompleteness is the disease, then I believe the answer, paradoxically, will need to have built into it *restless, lonely, incompleteness*—just as a serum has in it something of the *essence of the disease.* If our generation's problem is deeply personal, then the solution must be.

I am *not* equating being "personal" with being "individualistic." It seems to me this is a crippling misunderstanding—that "personal" faith implies "individualistic" behavior. Actually we can only be genuinely personal in relation to *other persons.* So a "social" program with lasting significance must be personal at the grass-roots level.

But how do we who have been trained to look victorious and adequate learn to bring our own inner problems and incompleteness into our communication of the gospel in a healthy, creative, and effective way? It's against everything some of us have been taught. In many seminaries (if not most) future ministers are told that it is bad taste, egotistical, and ineffective to speak personally in the sermon. I've heard ministers say from the pulpit, "Please excuse the personal illustration" when *they* are about to enter their own sermon for a moment. I can't help adding that it's lucky God didn't feel that way about a "personal illustration," or according to the Bible we wouldn't have even had Jesus Christ.

I understand the reticence ministers have about "being personal" and some of the past abuses which have caused it. My own training and education have stressed the importance of looking successful and happy and not talking about myself. And I believe in a positive enthusiastic approach to life and to communication.

But inside, I have been lonely somehow and have had terrific feelings of inadequacy. I've worried about what people thought of me (and denied that I cared). I have often been anxious about the future for myself and my children, frustrated in many of my close relationships, and I almost desperately avoid failure. And for years the rest of you out there in the world appeared to be very self-assured.

When God became more than just a word for me, I began to try to give him the keys to my future. At last I was not alone, and the deep restlessness began to subside. As I started to find out what God is like, I talked to some men and women around me about him. I tried to communicate with the self-assured people I saw, and nothing happened. Inwardly frustrated, I would sigh and go on alone, aching for someone to hear what I was hearing inside about personal freedom, hope, and a kind of belonging in the world. I was confused to realize that *I* could be finding a way to live that really turned me on, and yet all the approaches I'd been taught to *communicate* religious truth weren't getting across what I was experiencing. I wondered if anyone else felt stymied and rejected in trying to convey his deepest feelings about God.

I looked for books which would help me understand the strange inner contradictions in my life and my inability to move people toward God. I pored over the Scriptures and Christian classics. But only a few of the writers seemed to reveal their own inner contradictions so that I could study them—men like Paul and Augustine. And I had always thought of these men as "theologians." I hadn't realized that Paul may have been one of the first men to open himself in a personal way in his speaking and writing. He was often crude and in poor taste according to our ministerial standards: He bragged, saying in effect that he was the best Jew ever to come down the pike. Not only that but he implied that he was also the best Christian. He told some of his followers in detail how he'd suffered more by having been whipped, shipwrecked, and so on. (see 2 Cor. 11: 21–33.) And if they were ever in doubt about how to live for Christ, they could imitate *him* (Phil. 3:17). At one point Paul got angry and implied he didn't think Mark was good enough to go on his second missionary journey with him (Acts 15:37–39). He was blunt. And on one occasion he chewed Peter out in front of some of Peter's followers at a dinner at Antioch (Gal. 2:11–21).[1] Paul was frustrated by his inability to follow his own preaching—and he *told* us so (Rom. 7:15).

So much of the time Paul seems to have been talking about himself. And ironically he almost never quoted his Lord.[2] Every time Paul got in trouble he seems to have recited the account of his own personal encounter with Christ (for example, Acts 22:3–21; 26:4–23). Yet everywhere this strange man who loved Christ went, lives were transformed through contact with him. And, paradoxically, they became devoted to *Christ* and *not Paul*.

---

1. In this instance there was a very important matter of principle at stake. But I include it here because today almost *any* deep expression of anger or hostility is considered to be in bad taste in many churches.

2. Since the Gospel accounts in written form were probably not available to Paul, it is not surprising that he did not quote from them. But the point here is that the great apostle did pretty well in communicating the faith without having to "quote," when he spoke of Jesus and his work.

Why? when he talked about his own experience so much? When Paul opened his inner life with its conflicting love of his Lord on one hand and his desire to be the number one disciple on the other, what was there for his audiences to see? The *living* Christ was there! When Paul was vulnerable enough to open his life to others in a natural way, his audience could see the living God *at work,* healing and changing a lonely, miserable, and compulsive life *before their eyes*—and through Paul's vulnerability they sometimes found hope in their own misery. If God could do it for Paul, God might for them. They *identified!*[3]

Among those modern Christian groups which have continued the approach of "witnessing" about God's action in their own lives, there is a tendency to follow an unwritten "formula." This set pattern is very different from Paul's open, vulnerable style. The modern "standard brand church witness" mentions problems the speaker has *had* in the *past,* but they are almost always *old* problems and *solved* problems and *pre*-Christian problems. For example, "I used to beat my wife, drink too much, and cheat at cards—*until* I met Christ." The witness may then smile humbly, thereby implying that *now* he is pure and untroubled by temper, intemperance, and dishonesty—or by implication, anything else that is negative. But when a Christian brings out only these old dead sins, it's sometimes like dragging out a moldy stuffed hawk mounted in a live and threatening pose, dusting it, and showing it off

---

3. Anyone who may think Paul's honesty about his own existing unsolved problems was a departure from his biblical background should read the psalms. There the authors really lay out their hostilities and frustrations about life and God.

to people as a fierce adversary. Everyone knows it's not dangerous now. Its claws are still and its eyes are glass.

What Paul seems to have done in his meetings (and his letters) was to throw open the windows of his life and let some live sins or weaknesses fly out, feathers and all— some *real, current* problems that he was still struggling with. This way people could actually see God working in Paul's life, "catching" some of those problems and sins before their eyes. That was *first hand, contemporary* evidence to his audiences that God was alive.

Paul's courage, as a perfectionist Pharisee, in admitting that even in Christ he couldn't be whole must have seemed like a real miracle. A man without a great inner source of security could never have been so personally vulnerable to people who might have rejected and even harmed him. This vulnerable style communicated great power, though the content was often failure and weakness, beyond which Paul pointed to "hope."

This can be illustrated by a particular verse of Scripture which is sometimes quoted to indicate that the committed Christian need *not* reveal his personal problems. Paul is quoting our Lord as telling him, "My grace is sufficient . . ." But the same verse goes on to quote God as saying, ". . . my power is made perfect in weakness." And Paul concludes by stating that he will continue to speak of his weaknesses, ". . . that the power of Christ may rest upon me. For the sake of Christ, then, I am content with weaknesses . . . for when I am weak, then I am strong" (2 Cor. 12:9, 10). Paul found that when he knew *he* was weak and lacking in strength, the power of *God* could work through him *better*. And the great apostle had decided to *use his weaknesses as a part of his ministry—*

thus making it stronger! And this is the paradox of the personal, vulnerable approach.

But in the twentieth century we are terrified to open ourselves in this way. We are afraid because there is a paradox involved in this vulnerable style of communication. The speaker is free to illustrate current doubts and difficulties, as well as hope and meaning from his own life. But only *other* people can see *Christ* in the brokenness of *our* circumstances. We cannot.[4] All we can see are the unsolved problems in our lives. In our lack of faith we are afraid others will only see the awful truth about us. And we won't risk this, especially on a continuing basis.[5]

So we in the contemporary church preach "doctrinally correct" or "socially relevant" sermons. But these seldom give people direction or hope concerning their secret inner problems, which they fear others will discover and reject them for having. J. H. Oldham (1951, p. 88) tells us that Florence Allshorn and the people at St. Julian's Community found that "there is no peace, whatever kind of a facade they put on, for people who somewhere inside themselves have a fear of being known. They must break through this fear, no matter at what cost, if they are going to have any message for this generation."

---

4. Except occasionally in retrospect.
5. Using a personal approach does not mean doing away with the Scriptures or theological concepts. It means rather *blending* one's life into his preaching by illustrating problems and hopes one has experienced in the caldron of current living.

Five

The Power of the Personal: Identifying with the Problem

W HAT I think we are doing when we begin opening ourselves to each other with our true needs, hopes, dreams, and discoveries is to *identify* with the *"problem"* the gospel speaks to instead of the *"answer."* For years as a Christian I identified in my own mind with the answer. I was trained to do this in the church and in seminary. In all our communication strategy meetings *we* (with our message) represented the *answer* to the world's problems. The question was, how could we get the indifferent people in the world to stand still so that we could drop it on them—this message of living truth. But they never seemed to be listening. And most of them avoided our psychological attempts to catch them and mark them with our own particular brand of Christianity (so they could be right or do God's will, like us).

It was the late Richard Niebuhr who pointed out that

Jesus Christ identified with the problem, not the answer. As a matter of fact, Jesus identified so completely that the Pharisees could get away with "mistaking" him for a sinner. But what is meant by: "to identify with the problem"? At first this sounds like a denial of one's faith or commitment.

One night, several years ago, I was speaking to a group of church leaders in a local congregation, and we were stumped at this point. One man finally said, "I don't even know what you *mean*, identify with the *problem*. Do you want us to pretend we're *not* Christians?"

I thought a minute and asked, "How many of you men would go with me to a whore house tonight to witness for Jesus Christ?" After a moment there were a few hesitant hands or nods. "All right," I said, "how many of *you* would go alone and without a Bible?" If we go with Bibles or prayer books or tracts prominently displayed in our hands, they know we aren't really coming into their world. We aren't in any true sense one of them in their loneliness and misery. They know that we are only "Christmas-basket Christians," and that we won't even take the chance that people might think we are one of them. But, if a man is seen going into a "house of ill repute" without a Bible, he might be mistaken for a customer. And everyone knows the risk of this kind of vulnerability when they see it. But it's the risk that Jesus took.[1]

---

1. Different people respond to different approaches, and if a man is down and out *enough*, he may respond to a gospel of salvation even if it includes a seemingly unreal pious language and life-style. However, if a person is miserable but *still coping*, he must usually have some kind of identification with the communicator before he will "hear" him. In *any* case he will usually smell out the Christian do-gooder and reject him.

Alcoholics Anonymous found out a long time ago that only those who admit that they are *still* weak and powerless to handle alcohol on their own can help other alcoholics find new lives with self-respect. In the ghettos those who share the smell of urine on rotting tenement steps and who walk through the same garbage in the streets—those are the workers who have been most effective in the inner city and the Peace Corps and with kids. Men and women who become vulnerable enough to share the dangers and problems are those most likely to help set people free from those problems—and to communicate an authentic message of hope.

Jesus Christ "thought it not too great" to become vulnerable, to taste and feel and reveal to us the nature of the struggles of our own lives. Most people certainly do not think of Jesus as one who talked about his personal problems as a part of his ministry. But he did! He *must* have. As Bruce Larson (1972) has pointed out, if Jesus did not tell his disciples about the specific nature of his dilemmas with his own temptations, then how did they find out to write them down? The record indicates that none of them was with him in the wilderness, or in Gethsemane where he "sweated blood." Jesus told Peter, James, and John that he was troubled, fearful, and anxious. He must have told them *something* more of what happened (even though it isn't recorded) because they were all asleep during part of the action.[2]

In any case Christ shared his real life—the unpleasant

---

2. I am aware of the critical problem concerning the recording of the text from earlier oral materials. But it seems clear to me that the tradition of the early church substantiates the point of Jesus' sharing his problems, whatever one argues about the authenticity of certain specific sayings.

and the pleasant parts—with his disciples. Jesus' behavior reflected an amazing combination of almost defenseless vulnerability coupled with an inner source of apparently boundless personal power. And through this combination of weakness and strength an identifying force was made available which continues to unlock fearful men and women.

And when a Christian speaker identifies the problems to which he is speaking with his own experience, his listeners can hear and psychologically afford to admit that they experience the same difficulties. Then confession and healing can take place.

This may sound very improper or like a paradox to those who have been trained to avoid the use of personal material in preaching or teaching. And I realize that there may not be a single seminary in which this style or method is being taught today. But having tried the personal approach for over fifteen years and having taught it in a seminary as a guest lecturer, I am convinced that whatever the risks—some of us must put our own lives and difficulties where our communication is. My own experience indicates that personal healing and liberation have taken place among church members only when *someone* began this process of personal openness.

Countless times, however, I have seen that when the church loses vulnerable personal honesty from the pulpit, the Sunday school class, in elders' meetings, and in its prayers, then we are no longer personal in our congregations. And deep communication about the inner pilgrimage stops. Something of the gospel dies, and we can no longer speak to a frantic, depersonalized generation in its agony.

The dangers and excesses of public confession and

sharing are great and cannot be taken lightly. One should be very careful not to expose the people around him—in the name of honesty—without their permission. There is also the danger of expressing thoughts or relating experiences which unduly threaten or alarm your listeners —thus breaking communication. For example, a person can use public confession as a way to brag about his sins or to bolster his masculine identity. And there is a very real danger in becoming so enamored with "honesty" that the historical-biblical essence of the message about *God* and his redeeming love is forgotten. But in our small group we found that some of these pitfalls, and others, can be avoided through the honest interchange of a group of fellow-becomers. And we discovered very painfully that there *should* be some areas which are kept private to each person if he is to maintain his identity and integrity. I suppose I could write a short book on the "perils of being personal" from the mistakes I have already made.

But having said these things, I feel that the *need* for and the *power* of "the personal" are very great. And I believe that only a life-style in which confession and personal sharing are integral parts of one's ministry can break through many people's defensive filters into their isolated inner lives. We also discovered in our group that this cannot be only a "communication technique." It must be a *style of living and relating* if it is to have the leavening effect of being personal. And those who are vulnerable lead the way. As group therapist Raymond Corsini (1964, p. 42) has indicated, it has been shown time and again that the healing process and personal involvement in groups are accelerated immeasurably by those who will first risk honest sharing. He says that "there seems no doubt that any member can accelerate or decelerate the progress of others by his own movements. The more venturesome and courageous members advance the level or depth of therapy, while the more timid hold it back. Watching some members take chances in self-revelation impels others to do likewise." Seeing the increased freedom, personal assurance, and self-insight of some Christians gives others confidence.

In my enthusiasm I may appear to be saying that a "confessional" stance is the *only* live option for effective communication of the gospel. This is *not* true. *Most* of the greatest preachers and teachers alive will probably continue to proclaim the Christian message without ever becoming personally open and vulnerable from the pulpit or in small groups. But for some of us, the blending of relevant personal experience into our preaching and witnessing represents a new and powerful style of relating the gospel. And I guess my point is that without *some* group in a congregation actually trying to live and communicate the personal and vulnerable life, the most brilliant "objective" preaching in the world cannot create genuine Christian community in a world like ours.

Six

Being Open
As a Christian:
the Terror of Beginning

B UT how would a Christian start to open his life to others after years of being careful not to? With me it began in an unexpected way. Having made a beginning commitment of my life to God, I was teaching a Sunday school class of teen-agers and was beginning to pray and read the Scriptures. When I got up in the mornings, I was told to say, "Lord, I love you!" And I said it— whether I felt like it or not. But one morning I woke up and felt terrible. Tired of "being good" and of Christian people who were so victorious, I said, "God, I don't like you at all, and I wish you would get off my back and leave me alone. I'd like to go to Acapulco and have a runaway!" Then I lay there in bed waiting for lightning to strike. But no lightning. So I told God, "I don't *want* to feel this way about you, but that's the way it is right now." For the first time I had really leveled with God when I was very hostile toward him, and I felt that he understood. At that moment I began to be able to accept my feelings.

When one denies to himself a genuine feeling, like anger at his mother or God, often that feeling will come out as a neurotic fear of *something else,* or guilt, or bad dreams. But now I realized that God really could take my negative impulses, as well as my praise, and love me anyway. So I told him all about my secret resentments, lusts, *and hopes* even though I knew he was already aware of them. With great relief I began to get in touch with my true feelings about people, myself, and God, feelings which I'd repressed because they seemed unacceptable.[1] The discoveries were amazing to me. So many of my feelings had been repressed in order to fit the image of myself I thought would please my father and other people. But I began to offer these hidden feelings openly to God for change, shaping, and forgiveness.

These findings became painful but valuable ways to grow toward a sense of being all of one piece—not so fragmented, since I didn't have to avoid thinking about certain areas of my life so much. The present came alive. And I began to face issues as they were happening, instead of running away to other places and times in my mind. As I was reading one of the letters of Pierre Teilhard de Chardin (1962), I realized that although travel and history help correlate knowledge, that the truth about life does not exist out there nor back there. But it exists in coming to grips with the problems of life *as they are taking place.* The sweat of fear and the steaming fog of anxiety sometimes blind me, but they mingle with my conclusions

---

1. In my case my deeply *positive* feelings about myself had been as unacceptable as the negative ones.

about events and give them deeper significance as they relate to Life and Death.

Now my communication took on a new quality. I didn't have to be so careful not to make a mistake, and I could laugh at myself more. If I blew it, I had a place to go inside my mind with *all* my experiences and problems— though I still cringe and want to die when I make a bad mistake and look inadequate or naïve. As this accepting and confessing to God of unacceptable feelings started, my whole life began to expand. I found myself *wanting* to find and do God's will as it related to other people with a growing excitement. At last I knew he was interested in the gutsy, painful parts of life.

As I reread the Scriptures, I began to see that they are filled with the ruggedness and struggles of actual life. But in our teaching of the gospel we have sweetened or repressed the universal human qualities of our Lord's stories almost beyond recognition. Jesus evidently talked about things like people's sexual escapades (for example, John 4:6–30; 8:3–11; Luke 15:11–32),[2] and crooked business deals (Matt. 21:33–41) to illustrate his message about the reign of God. And he is reported to have furnished additional wine for at least one celebration (John 2:1–11).

Read the parables. With the whole of human behavior from which to select, Jesus *chose* the gritty, earthy areas of life to illustrate the way God loves people. He was *real!* He expressed his own uncertainty and doubt in the midst of his faith (Matt. 26:39; 27:46). And he got very

2. I am aware of the problem of lumping together sayings of Jesus from the fourth Gospel with those of the synoptics. But in this book I am dealing with the church's traditional view concerning Jesus' sayings and behavior, which was derived largely before or without regard to the critical problems concerning authorship.

angry (Matt. 21:12, 13; 23:13–36). Louis Cassels (1968, p. 93) quotes Professor John Knox as saying that "no account of Jesus could be even approximately correct which did not call attention to his frequent and sudden anger."

I began to see that if we can sweep away the accumulated "historical sugar" we discover that Jesus was talking about the same deep separation, dishonesty, and inner restlessness we experience in modern life. I had always heard the church saying that God prefers the poor, the despised, and the weak. But now I was beginning to understand what Paul Tournier (1962, p. 114) meant when he said, "What religious people have much more difficulty in admitting, is that He prefers sinners to the righteous." This is the biblical viewpoint and is confirmed by modern psychology: All men are equally burdened with guilt. Those who call themselves righteous are not free from it but have repressed it. Those called sinners are aware of their guilt and are, for that reason, ready to receive pardon and grace. And yet I could not see the reason for Christ's special closeness with us sinners until I really leveled with God about *my own* dishonesty, negative feelings, and doubts, even about *him*.

Out of this first honest and therefore desperately personal communication with God began to develop a new kind of relationship with him. I am convinced now that honesty *about one's self* and "personalness" are highly correlated. A personal friend is one who knows what I am like and loves me anyway.

Some people have misunderstood and thought we are saying that personalness is created by a raw and uninhibited honesty *about other people* and their behavior. But I am saying that one begins with a vulnerable honesty about himself and his own behavior. In the small-group movement there seem to be two distinct approaches to breaking through people's facades. It's almost as if we were chickens trapped in our shells. One way to break the shell is with a hammer. That has been very effective with tough birds, but you may have some crippled and helpless chicks on your hands. The other way is to create an atmosphere of safety and warmth (through confession) in which the "chicken" can come out from the inside at his own speed. The ratio of healthy chicks seems higher. And this is the approach of most becomers' groups.

But in my own journey, I find truly vulnerable honesty with other people to be very difficult. At first I was only honest with God in the privacy of my prayers. I was still afraid that if *other* Christians knew what I was thinking behind my Christian facade they wouldn't accept me—just as I have always secretly suspected that if anyone got close enough to *really* know me, they would walk away and leave me. But then came a miracle. One day in a counseling situation, in order to identify with a man who was really suffering from guilt, this inner honesty accidentally spilled over into my outer life.

The man confessed a problem in a close relationship which reflected an attitude he definitely considered to be un-Christian. He was a very sensitive person, and his rejection of himself for having these feelings was intense. After his confession I looked at him for a long minute; he seemed so lonely with his problem—and I was horrified to realize that I had the *same difficulty that morning.* I was tempted to pray for him and keep still about my problem. Actually I just wanted to get away. But since I couldn't, I found myself sort of sheepishly telling the man in his misery that I had experienced the same kind

of jealousy and hostile resentment he had *that same day.*
I thought he would walk out of my office in disgust.
But instead, he just looked at me in disbelief and said,
"Are you serious?" Then I really wished I hadn't told
him. But when I nodded my head, he began to weep and
said, "Oh, *thank* you. If you've got this problem and are
able to keep going as a committed Christian, maybe I
can. I have been so *alone.*" I remember being very surprised
at his reaction and realizing that he hadn't primarily
wanted an "answer man." He had wanted someone
to be *with him* in his problem. And my identification
with him as a "sinner" was a kind of "answer" from his
perspective—since we were *side by side* before God in
need of grace and forgiveness.

As I am writing this, I remember a story Paul Rees
once told about a priest who went to minister in a leper
colony on an island in the Pacific. For months the man
couldn't get to first base in communicating the gospel.
Then one day it was discovered that he had contracted
leprosy. The word spread through the colony. The following morning the chapel was filled with lepers, and a wave
of conversions took place. When they *knew* he understood their dominant problem *personally,* they could hear
his message of hope.

As I began to share my inner life, I started to experience a whole new dimension of communication and relatedness with God and with people—all kinds of people.
And as I became more personal in pointing to God, some
of the men and women I talked to began to believe and
have hope. By confessing my humanity *as a committed
Christian,* I had joined those with whom Christ lived
and came to heal—those who *know* they need a physician

(see Mark 2:15–17). And all it cost me was my reputation—*with Christians who have no problems.*

But to speak to those who realize that they have unsolved difficulties, I have found that the natural earthy language of life can be combined with a vulnerable willingness to illustrate current perplexities from your own experience. And if these problems relate to active needs in your listeners' inner lives, the hope and meaning of the gospel can become *more* instead of less believable to them.[3]

In our small group we finally had discovered that we could be personal, and communication had improved a great deal. But it soon became apparent that we all had inner difficulties we did not understand—and were still afraid to admit. We saw that we really didn't know much about what might go on in the "normal" human mind, behind the masks we show to each other. I began to look at the Scriptures through the lens of psychology to try to understand what kinds of inner forces operate to cause the anguish and sense of conflict we all experienced . . . even as committed Christians.

------

3. One certainly walks a tightrope in taking this approach. I think the dangers of using this sort of freedom irresponsibly are enormous. But I believe the need and the results can be worth a lot of risking.

Question II

What's Inside

Behind Our Masks?

Seven

The Unseen Warfare

ONE of the most exciting things about the becomers is their belief that *all* truth is a part of God's scheme. And if we are committed to him and to each other, we do not have to be afraid of what we may find inside ourselves—that in fact, knowing this truth will help to make us free.

As far back as I can remember, a lot of my own behavior and that of the people around me has been frustrating and simply did not make sense. For instance, when I am lonely or feel a great lack of self-worth, I want most to be loved by my wife. But I often strike out at her at such times and make it almost impossible for her to love me.

At other times I feel guilty when I have done something I do not consciously think is wrong. Sometimes I become anxious about my vocational future even when my prospects are brightest.

Although I do not believe in doing things to butter up the wealthy and influential, I catch myself flattering such people and *needing* to be accepted by them. This is true even though I don't even want to be an integral part of their world and life-style.

Sometimes I am driven to succeed in ventures which don't interest me. For instance, in school I worked very hard for A's in some classes when I didn't like either the teacher or the subject. And I remember arguing with myself as if there were more than one person inside my head. I'd hear myself say, "You don't really *care* about this course and you know it. Why don't you just get by and spend the extra time on subjects which are really important to you and your future?" But then another side of me (often very unreasonably, it would seem) might answer, "But you *ought* to do well in this class. I'm counting on you to do well." It was as if there were a strange war going on inside me—with different parts of me wanting different things in the same situation.

And this war is intensified when I want to do something that I was taught as a child was wrong. At other times when there is apparently *no* battle going on at all and everything seems serene, I am sometimes overwhelmed by a temptation and succumb to it—almost in amazement at myself.

Because of my counseling experience and the thousands of anonymous responses to questions which I have collected over the past eight years, I am assuming that these are struggles some of you have faced. Or perhaps they may be real for people to whom you are trying to communicate a gospel of wholeness. So I would like to talk about this war that seems to go on inside us. In the following chapters I am going to try to describe one picture or model of the inner mind which has helped me to understand more about what may go on in the lives of people to whom I'm talking—not to mention my own. The Scriptures are filled with accounts and descriptions of the strange battles going on within its heroes' lives. Look at Saul's great ambivalence about his relationship to David. King Saul called David into his court, gave him a favored position, and loved him like his own son, Jonathan (1 Sam. 16:21). And the next thing we know Saul was throwing a spear, trying to pin David against the dining room wall (1 Sam. 18:11). Then came remorse and an oath not to kill David (1 Sam. 19:6). But then an "evil spirit" would come upon Saul, and he would throw another spear, almost against his own will it seemed, and certainly against his word (1 Sam. 19:9, 10). He was driven back and forth by his inner conflict.

David, although not appearing to be nearly as neurotic as Saul, had wars and contradictions of all kinds going on inside himself. And with great honesty the writers of the Bible spelled out the results of these inner struggles. Here was David, the great man of God, the prototype of the Messiah, Jesus Christ. David evidently wanted very much to be God's person. He longed to be Yahweh's representative to the nations, and he was. He defeated the Philistines, brought the ark home to Jerusalem, and made his capital the City of God. He accomplished these and many other remarkable achievements in building the kingdom. But in the midst of his rise to international power, he looked out the window one day and saw Bathsheba taking a bath. He sent for her, slept with her, and got her pregnant. Then he compounded his crime by having her husband Uriah murdered so that he could

escape being caught as an adulterer and still have
Bathsheba (2 Sam. 11:2–24). It didn't fit his image or
his game plan to do a cowardly, sneaky thing like that.
He proved it by his later actions. But he *did* these unacceptable things in the *midst* of his greatness as a man
of God.

This sort of strange conflict went on inside men all
through the Bible, and they didn't understand it. But,
unlike most of us, the biblical writers were honest enough
to describe their heroes' struggles and their own.

We often tend to think of the kinds of conflicting and
alternating behaviors in people like David and Saul as
happening to men of God only in the Old Testament,
before men had "Christ and the Holy Spirit." But the
New Testament is filled with its witness to the opposing
forces *within* man's make-up. Paul faced this unseen warfare as much as any other man in the Bible, and he was
perhaps the most perceptive person in the New Testament among the early followers of Christ. Let's look at a
partial paraphrase of the seventh chapter of Phillips'
translation of Paul's letter to the Romans. "My own
behavior baffles me, because I find myself doing what I
really don't want to do, but what I actually loathe. But
if I do the things that I really don't want to do, I am
admitting that I agree with the law. But it can't be said
that *I* am doing them. *I* am not doing them at all. It must
be sin that has made its home in my nature (and indeed
I know from experience that the carnal side of my being
can scarcely be called the home of good).

"I often find that I really want to do good, but I don't
have the power. That is, that I don't accomplish the good
that I set out to do, and the evil that I don't really want
to do, that's the thing I find I am doing. And then if I

do the things that I really don't want to do, it is not, I repeat, 'I' who do them. It must not be. It is sin that has made its home within me. When I come up against the law, I want to do good and yet I practice evil. My conscious mind wholeheartedly endorses the law and yet I observe an entirely different principle down there somewhere working inside my nature. This is in continual conflict with my conscious attitude and makes me an unwilling prisoner inside. In my mind I am God's willing servant, but in my own nature I am bound fast, as I said, to the law of sin and death. It's an agonizing situation for a Christian to be in, and who on earth can set me free from this strange war and the clutches of my own sinful nature?" (see Rom. 7:15–24).

This describes my condition exactly. I want to be a fine Christian but am continually resentful, selfish, and thoughtless—often when I least want to be.

But I'm not helped much when I look at other people. We all *seem* to be struggling with different problems— even within the same family. Children with the same parents often have very different life-styles. Why is it that some people are driven to be neat housekeepers and others couldn't care less? Why do some men and women become beachcombers and others compulsive drinkers, or compulsive ministers? Why are we restless and guilty when we can't see a reason for these feelings? When we seem to have everything we need, sometimes we are restless. What are the strange fears and rumblings that we wake up with in the middle of the night when we can't see anything to be afraid of? What is this war? What goes on inside our minds in these dark areas behind the veil where we can only feel and hear what's happening but can't locate the source of the struggle?

Christ said that out of the heart come things which get us in trouble (Mark 7:21, 22). Paul had real trouble understanding his behavior because he couldn't pull up the rock and look into the *unconscious* part of his inner life. He didn't know it existed—though in his honesty he described its activities very graphically.

As our small group began to feel safer, we took some psychological tests together.[1] And we discovered all kinds of things about our unconscious behavior which had stopped us from loving people and them from loving us. Part of the problem was inordinate self-centeredness or "sin." But many of us had not realized that *much* of the anxious feeling and inner warfare we experienced was *not* sin at all but a *normal* part of trying to cope in a threatening world. We realized that it would be very helpful to know more about the recurring struggles which go on inside our heads.

───────

1. These tests are distributed by Yokefellows, Inc. in Burlingame, California.

Eight

The Inner Stage:
a Picture of the Human Mind

T HE next few chapters represent a decided change of
pace, but please stay with me.

To grasp and communicate a gospel which claims to
offer healing to the total man, some knowledge of our
unconscious life seems to me to be essential. Please don't
misunderstand; I am *not* trying to slip Sigmund Freud
into the Christian community. I disagree heartily with
many of his conclusions about personality development
and certainly with some of his theological statements.[1]

---

1. Among other things I don't agree with his notion that God
is only a projection of a human father, nor do I believe in the
universality of the Oedipal complex and that all neuroses have
their source in infant sexuality. For further information on Freud's
theories see listing under his name in the References.

Some contemporary students, particularly "third force" or Gestalt
psychologists, feel that the id, ego, and superego model is outmoded
and perpetuates the split mind fallacy. I agree that man's per-

But anyone who tries to examine the whole content of the mind has got to deal with what Freud discovered. So to get some sort of picture of what may happen inside us, let me do something that would make Freud roll over in his grave. I am going to try to describe some of the basic dynamics of our mental activity as a "drama."

What this approach does for me is to clarify part of what Paul meant when he talked about an inner warfare. It's only one picture of the mind, and it's fragmented and oversimplified. But I think it is basically true to Freud and to human experience.

A "Picture" of the Inner Stage

Freud thought that all mental activity was a result of the interaction of certain forces in our lives. If you were asleep and nothing interrupted you, you might lie in bed forever. But the pressure of hunger or some other physiological need begins to nudge you awake and finally forces you to get up. Besides physiological pressures, there are

---

sonality is not divided into separate parts but is a single whole. And although I am closer in spirit and therapeutic methodology to the humanistic psychologists, I have used one part of the Freudian model in this section for the following reasons: 1. Man's mind may not be divided into discrete parts, but our *experience* is that we *are* divided within ourselves. And in some symbolic way the id, ego, and superego "warfare" seems to me to express some of the conflict experienced by Christians more clearly than a Gestalt model, for instance. 2. Although some academic psychologists may not agree that one *can* be eclectic enough to get some of Freud's symbols under the same umbrella with some of Maslow's, I disagree. Psychology is in such a primitive state as compared to other sciences that I believe we must make use of those bits and pieces of clarity which shed any light on human behavior—realizing the great lack of completeness in all personality theories.

also mental forces at work, sometimes going in opposite directions from the physiological.

What are these forces?

First I'd like to draw a rough picture of an "empty" human mind. (See figure 1 by turning to fold- out pictures on page 88 which can be left open while reading chapters eight through eleven.) Figure 1 is just a circle. But this picture represents the "stage" or the "house" in which we live out the inner drama of our days and nights. This is the empty stage. The part at the top, above the dotted line, is our *conscious* mind. In this "area" are the things we see and feel and of which we are conscious. Then there is the part below the conscious (below the dotted line in the picture but above the solid line) which is called the *preconscious*. In this area are the things that are not conscious right now, but which we could *make* conscious with relatively little difficulty.

Here is an example of how this could work. Right now there are hundreds of things going on that you are aware of at a preconscious level. But if you are concentrating on these words, you are not thinking about most of the other things which are happening. Now, let me make you conscious of one of these preconscious feelings. Concentrate on the pressure of the chair against your backside. Can you feel it now? Isn't that strange? The same pressure was there a minute ago, but you may not have been conscious of it (and now you may have trouble not thinking about it). That feeling was preconscious, but when I called your attention to it, it became conscious. I could name a dozen things just like this, and suddenly you could pull them up in your conscious life above the dotted line in the picture.

But by far the greatest part of our mental life is *un-*

conscious and relatively inaccessible to us. (See the part below the solid line in fig. 1.) Freud thought of the conscious part of the mind as being like the tip of an iceberg, most of which is out of our "sight" or consciousness. From the first time we can see, hear, smell, taste, or touch we start "storing" feelings, images, and sensations. Some of these memories and impressions we can recall, and they are stored in the preconscious area. But some are so painful and threatening that we "repress" them. Or, in other words, without being aware that we are doing it, we push them past the preconscious clear down into the basement or unconscious area of our minds so we can *not* recall them at will. But these "repressed" thoughts and feelings stay "alive." And frequently they slip into our consciousness in dreams (sometimes in wild costumes and unrecognizable disguises) when we are asleep and cannot sit on the "lid" to the unconscious area of our lives.[2]

But besides repressed material, think of the large lower area of figure 1 as containing free-floating psychic energy —the "wind which fills the sails of behavior." Often strong driving forces, many of which we don't consciously understand, control our emotional life. Some of these drives take on conscious form in such things as the irrational push to be successful, the pressing need to be right, or to be the man of the house. Sometimes out of

2. Note that "repression" differs from "suppression" in that suppression is the conscious putting things out of mind. These can be recalled at will, and this is healthy. But unconscious repressed material cries out to be noticed and makes us anxious "over nothing" since we cannot see or recall *what it is* we have repressed. To study the way Freud thought repression operates to keep repressed material from consciousness, see Freud's (1960) *General Introduction to Psychoanalysis,* chap. 19.

our unconscious comes the awful fear of being left alone in the world or the strong drive for sex during inappropriate times or circumstances. These feelings and many more are conscious to us but their sources or *reasons for being* are unconscious.

The "Actors" in the Inner Drama

Now look at the drawing underneath (fig. 2, p. 88). This is the picture of the mind "inhabited" by a real person. At first it would seem that the house of the mind is full of people. The first picture of the divided circle (fig. 1) is the human mind roughly as Freud saw it. Actually he did not have any diagrams that look like this second drawing. That is a picture from my own imagination, but it helps me to see the inner "struggle" of the forces Freud described most vividly. The *unconscious,* which is the great lower part with the blind giant in it, is the world of unseen forces which exercises bewildering control over our conscious thoughts. The *preconscious,* the little crosshatched strip, is halfway between the conscious and the unconscious. And the conscious is the smallest area at the top of the circle.

Now, instead of one person inside of you, imagine a small family of three orphan brothers. *Don't misunderstand me;* I am *not* saying that there are three people inside us, nor was Freud. He is often misunderstood this way. But these three little people represent three often conflicting *forces* which seem to struggle to dominate all our actions. However, I am going to talk about them *as if* they were three orphan brothers, members of a small family with *very* different interests.

Nine

Members of the "Inner Family"

I might as well tell you about the "shame" of the family first.

The Id

Id, the oldest and most primitive brother, lives in the basement. He's blind, musclebound, and we—especially we Christians—try to hide him from the world. Even though he's perfectly normal, we've chained him in the basement and locked the door. Id's activities are often an embarrassment to the whole family since he seems to be so self-centered and totally uninhibited. He embodies our basic instincts and everything psychological that is inherited. Representing the inner world of subjective experience, he has no knowledge of the outside world of objective reality. Id lives down in the physiological and psychological basement. He's the reservoir of energy which motivates our actions. Id also activates us to meet our most basic needs for survival. These are nonrational needs; they are things we must have, like food and sexual expression. For example, if we get hungry, the need is signaled to Id in the basement through physiological processes. And this "need" makes Id "nervous and tense." The tension is like heat down there, and he starts rattling his chains and poking up into the conscious to get us to do something to reduce that tension.

Our conscious experience of this activity is a feeling of hunger, for instance, or a desire for sexual contact. In any case Id starts making an internal fuss because he cannot tolerate increases in tension. So when the body has certain basic needs, Id starts making us restless and getting our conscious attention. His "aim" is to get us to discharge the tension by getting the body some food or a sex object, or whatever will meet the need signaled to him. Id becomes increasingly frantic to get our conscious attention since he wants to "rest" from the "pressure" caused by the need. He lives only for this pleasure of discharging tension. (Freud called this the "pleasure principle.")

Id is totally amoral and self-centered. He doesn't care whether getting relief hurts anyone, destroys other people's property, or even endangers the whole body. But without this "signaling" function to make us consciously aware of our needs, we would not meet them and we'd die.

Besides these signals to our consciousness, there are certain actions that are unconscious and automatic which are called "reflex actions." For instance, try not to blink for three minutes. We blink anyway. We blink because that gives us pleasure and prevents pain. If we didn't blink, our eyes would get raw and painful and cause Id tension. But it all happens unconsciously. The same with a sneeze: If we start to block our air passages (which would kill us), we are compelled to sneeze by reflex action. These are some of the functions that are controlled from Id's unconscious realm.

The Ego

But Id has a problem: If he experiences a need (or tension) down there, how is he going to get it satisfied? He is locked in the basement and can't see anything in the outside world. He only "feels" things happening inside us. So the way he gets the body's basic needs met is something like this: First the tension rises for Id. Then he starts "rattling his chains" and getting our attention.

Now comes the second brother or part of our personality, which in the picture is the man looking in on the side. His name is Ego. He's the middle brother. He can "see" the outside world and also the workings of the mind, except for unconscious material. Ego is the "us," the conscious us, the part of us which thinks, sees, smells, hears, and so on. Ego is sort of the executive of the body. He is not as old as Id, who represents the animal needs, but Ego can think. And Ego is the go-between representing the body with its basic needs in the world outside the body. He is the one who "decides" how to go out and get the satisfying essentials that the body needs. And ideally, Ego decides which needs are going to be satisfied at a given time.

What happens is that Id can communicate only up into the conscious to Ego. He can't communicate to the outside world. So, he starts rattling the chains when we are hungry, for instance. This disturbance to our consciousness is as if he put up a big memory picture of a steak on a kind of closed circuit television screen which (forgive me, Freud, wherever you are) Ego can "see." [1] Ego recognizes something is not serene and says to himself, "Something is wrong." Looking over at the screen, he sees the picture of the steaks and says, "Um, I'm hungry." So then Ego starts checking around in whatever environment we are in at the time. His job is to find something out in the real world that *matches* the *need* he's been signaled. If he sees food on the screen, he looks for food. If he sees sex as the need, he looks for a sex object.

What happens is that Ego can locate these objects in the world and match them with the inner need because he can "see" through the *body's* senses. So it is a team operation. Id says for the body, "I'm hungry. I don't care what it is; I want to eat it." And Ego says, "Wait a minute. We've got to find something edible." Ego is realistic. He lives by the "reality principle." He doesn't just blindly go after things as Id would have him do. He's got to protect the body from destruction while he's meeting its needs.

The way this works is very strange. If Id, which also represents primitive man, just forced us to go out and get what he wanted to reduce tension, we wouldn't last long because it is often dangerous out in the world. For example, imagine that we are watching a cave man named George. Because of his primitive state, he is practically all id. Now, George's physiological need for sex stirs

1. Freud called this forming of a memory image of that object which would reduce the tension "wish fulfillment," and the process through which Id attempts to reduce tension and avoid pain: the "primary process" (see Hall and Lindzey, 1957, p. 33).

within him. His id starts sending up signals, and George responds by saying to himself, "George wants sex. Jim, in the cave next door, has a good-looking mate. I'll go drag Jim's woman out and have a little sex." So he stalks over to Jim's cave, takes Jim's wife by the hair, and starts dragging her out of the cave. But Jim, built like Tarzan, is standing by the door with a club. And just as George goes by, Jim lets him have it over the head. When George wakes up several hours later, he says to himself (his ego says to him), "Don't take Jim's wife—*while Jim's at home.*" You see, George is not yet *moral*—just reasonable.

With the emergence of Ego, *rational* man is born. He is not yet thinking it is *wrong* to take Jim's wife. He is thinking, "Man, be careful *when* you do it." Ego is still trying to get our needs met and stay safe. This is rational man in our day, or any day. This predominantly rational stage is part of our development as individuals and as a people.

So Ego lives by the reality principle. He stops Id and puts the lid on our physical needs long enough to meet them properly and intelligently if at all possible. This rational process is the difference between man and some animals. And through it Ego controls the gateway to action, ideally.

But Ego has a problem because he lives in continual conflict with Id. Big brother is always saying, "*Now!* I am hungry and I want it *now!* And I don't care about the consequences." And Ego has got to say, "Now, wait a minute. Let's see if it's reasonable to meet the need now and in this way." But Id puts a lot of pressure on Ego for immediate gratification of felt needs. So here's part of the conflict and war that is going on within us continually:

the raw physical demands having to be curbed by reason. But there is more trouble . . . a lot more.

The Superego

To complete the personality family there is a little brother. And this is the one who gives most of us fits, particularly us Christians. Let me describe how he might come into the picture.

Imagine yourself sitting in church, you are about to go forward for the Lord's Supper, and there is a beautiful girl who comes down the aisle in a clinging jersey dress. She has no bra on—or so it would seem. You are sitting there looking and feeling very pious. And all of a sudden when you see the girl, a physiological need is aroused. Id gets the signal and starts rattling the chains down in the basement. When your body sends him the signal, you can almost hear Id giving an appreciative whistle. And Ego says, "Shut up, you're in church. It's *dangerous* to whistle in here. Someone may hear you!" And then another little voice says, "Aren't you *ashamed* of yourself? I thought you were too good a Christian to feel like that at a time like this—*just before communion!*"

And the third and youngest brother has appeared: The Superego or the conscience—the smug little guy in the attic at the upper left side of figure 2 on page 88. Superego is the last to be "born" in the individual personality and in the development of men in societies.

These then are the three brothers in our inner family of forces. At least the way they learn to fight, they certainly *act* like brothers.

Ten

Brothers
Will Be Brothers—
the Inner Feud Develops

T HIS is the progression in a child's life: Children and little babies are practically "all id," and they all "want it *now*," whatever it is. And if they can, they grab it and take it. Then, so that they can learn to live safely as adults, children (their egos) are educated to be rational. A child burns his hands on the stove and says to himself, "Hey, I'm not supposed to touch that because I'll get hurt."

But we also educate children by *rewards* and *punishments*. We teach them what is "right" and what is "wrong" in our opinion as parents. And our saying "good girl!" or "bad boy!" or spanking the child, begins to program the "little brother" upstairs (see figure 2). According to Freud, the superego or conscience arrives empty in the world. And a person's values and moral guidelines are programed into his superego by the people who raise him and by the society into which he is born. According to

Freud these values are basically fixed by the time we're about five years old.[1]

Superego acts as if its values are *absolute* rules, whereas these "truths" are actually a *five-year-old's interpretation of his parents' values* or of the society which raised him. Unfortunately, the parents often imply that *they* are able to keep the "rules" perfectly. They cannot. But a five-year-old child does not know this, so he thinks his parents are much "stronger" than they actually are. And to complicate matters Superego demands that the child "also" achieve absolute perfection. The false assumption on the part of the youngster about his parents' perfection leads to additional guilt when he grows up and doesn't understand why he cannot keep rules *perfectly*. So most children are raised with a lot of false guilt (in addition to "normal guilt," which is triggered by willful disobedience, and so on). And Superego knows nothing about *forgiveness*. He keeps punishing Ego for his failure to be perfect by Superego's standards. He's interested only in the "good name" of the "family."

I remember, in our small group, being amazed when I realized that I had been trained as a child to expect my behavior to be *perfect*. This had made me almost continually disappointed in myself—even if my performance happened to be superior. Almost all of us in the group began to see that feelings about our abilities and sense of worth were greatly distorted because of our battles to please (or ignore) a powerful superego.

It is quite possible that through inadequate training

---

1. Most contemporary psychologists (even neo-Freudian) would stress the importance of society's influence more than I appear to be doing here. For simplicity, I am using the term "parent," realizing that many other factors help shape the superego's values.

children may misunderstand society's guidelines and acquire twisted values, and their superegos will give them unhealthy signals.

A tragic situation exists in thousands of Christian homes today. Since some Christian parents do not believe in paddling, they discipline their children by giving or withholding love. A child is rewarded and punished by his parents, giving him love for "good" behavior or withholding love from him when he is "bad." His superego may become so programed that "bad" is whatever displeases people and "good" becomes that behavior which "makes people love me." The child may lose touch with *his own real needs* and desires and "repress" them because they seem to be "bad," that is: will make his parents not love him.

Death from "Overgoodness"

It often happens that a child may become so afraid of losing his parents' love that he tries to please them completely. In the process of repressing his own natural desires and feelings he may become trapped in a web of his parents' peculiarities. By the time the child is an adult, he may be living his whole life as his parents want him to. And the rest of the church and the world are unaware that this grown man has no freedom, no life of his own, and is a secret captive to an unnatural guilt.

This is the perfect Christian paradox. The parents are trying to be good and make the child into a fine Christian. Everything looks normal; no crime was intended; there is no corpse, no guilt. But what has happened? The child has been rejected. At least he *feels* rejected, not only by them, but by himself. He has been taught subtly that his true self must be evil if it doesn't conform to his parents' vision of what he should be. What has he lost? Just the one true and vital part of himself—his own yes-feeling, which is his very capacity for growth, his root system.

But he is not dead. "Life" goes on, and so must he.· From the moment he gives himself uncritically to doing his parents' will as an adult, the course has been set to create and maintain a false self.[2]

But this is not an authentic self; it is a self without wishes. He finds himself telling a person that he loves him, when in fact he despises him. He acts strong and enthusiastic when he feels weak and disinterested. And life is very grim as he goes through these motions—hoping not to be found out. But his movements are caricatures of living. And he does not perform them for love or joy but for psychic survival. For if he does not perform and please his superego, he fears his guilt will overwhelm him, he will not be loved, and will wind up deserted and alone.

This sort of trap is not life—not his life—it is a defense mechanism against death. It is also the machine of spiritual death, even if it takes place in a minister's or bishop's child. For such a person will be torn apart by repressed needs or paralyzed by partially conscious conflicts. Every motion, every reaction, is eroding and canceling out his being, his integrity. All the while he is disguised as a normal Christian and expected to behave like one! It seems that he can never be the unique, creative person God had in mind for him to be. And he doesn't even know what has happened to him since he is repressing his true self.[3]

---

2. For an excellent discussion of this point see elaboration by psychiatrist Karen Horney (1949).
3. Parents, of course, must teach their children values, and much

Repression, Ego's "Unfair Weapon"

Freud described this "repressing" as pushing thoughts "out of sight" into our "unconscious" without realizing that we are doing it. As indicated in chapter 8, this happens when some thought or memory is very threatening to Ego. The thought may be threatening because it is unacceptable to Superego. If the unacceptable thought became *conscious*, the superego (like an inner parent) would raise so much hell that there could be an all out war between Id, Ego, and Superego. And that might incapacitate the whole inner "family." So by what appears to be a mental "slight of hand" trick, the thought is repressed by Ego into the unconscious before we become fully aware of it.

But as I mentioned earlier, these repressed thoughts or feelings do not die. They often make themselves felt in an indirect way through physical symptoms or mannerisms —like aching arms, nervous coughs, constricted throat, or burning stomach. And the symptom becomes a disguise or decoy to lure the conscious mind away from the unacceptable thought. But this process takes its toll in terms of energy. To say it another way, it's as if the repressed desires and thoughts were something like buoyant beach balls which have been forced under water. It sometimes takes a lot of energy and concentration to keep

---

of every child's training involves rewards and punishments of some kind. Perhaps most of the culture poured into the average child's superego is beneficial. One good argument for the traditional family unit is that in a family the child is exposed to several different continuing and developing interpretations of the values of the society in which he is raised. But the point here is that some parents are not aware of the child's tremendous needs for their approval, and that he will sometimes even sacrifice his only hope for an authentic life in order to keep their rules.

them from bobbing to the surface. And so in our perverse human fear of seeing the truth about our feelings, we unconsciously cripple ourselves in many ways with neurotic symptoms. For example, if a Christian minister were sexually attracted to his own daughter, this would be so unacceptable to his superego that the thought would most likely be quickly repressed *before* it became conscious to the minister. But, as a result of the still active but repressed thought, the minister might find that he was suddenly and mysteriously impotent sexually with his wife, or that he was becoming very cold and distant in his relationships with his female parishioners. Both of these unconscious reactions to the repressed material would protect him from conflict or from "doing anything about" his totally unacceptable repressed thought.[4] But they would also make him unable to relate naturally to women.[5]

Freud described these and many other ways by which we defend ourselves from the superego's reaction to our unacceptable thoughts. They are called "defense mechanisms" of the ego.[6] And if we have never had some natural way to confess our unacceptable desires and still be loved, these defense mechanisms can make us excessively anxious and emotionally unnatural . . . lest we be found out. This accounts partially for the tremendous sense of relief

---

4. It is fascinating that the physical neurotic symptom is often related to the repressed thought (e.g., the minister's impotence. Of course there are also other causes of such impotence).

5. Freud would have probably looked for the original cause of the problem in a repressed incestuous wish in the minister's childhood concerning his mother. But most contemporary psychologists would not.

6. For an excellent brief discussion of these defenses see Hall and Lindzey (1957, p. 49) or Freud (1960, revised).

many of us in our particular group have felt at being able to confess our unacceptable fears and anxieties. And the more of them we are able to confess, the more we see that we had not seen before. And, paradoxically, as I confess and *am still accepted,* I feel *more* instead of *less* value as a person.

So in order to keep the family war from getting too fearful, Ego finds defensive ways to deceive his brothers (and himself). And since Ego can never please Id or Superego completely, he develops vague or acute feelings of failure and guilt—with no way to gain the inner love and forgiveness his situation cries out for. As experiences of failure and guilt pile up with no way to get rid of them, a child can begin to feel so unworthy that he cannot believe or accept anyone's love—even God's.

And until a developing child receives *some* affirmation which he *can* accept from someone, his so-called commitments and relationships may be only shadows or imitations of his parents' commitments or relationships. People who have come into the church on their parents' commitments often feel very uneasy about their faith. And they are not generally anxious to share their "inner feelings" with other church members.

In fact it seems that a person must have developed some sense of being an independent person *before he has a self* to commit to God. As Paul Tournier (1968) has pointed out, we do a great harm when we demand that children feel worthless and offer themselves as slaves to Christ *before* they have had a chance to experience their own independence and self-will *apart* from their parents' will. Such a commitment can hardly be healthy and liberating since the child's real self has not yet even tasted the independence it is supposedly committing to God.

Eleven

The Need for Something
Within—and Yet Beyond Us

IN this struggle for balance between our inner drives some of us have an almost desperate need for approval—perhaps not from the crowd but from someone *inside* us. We seem to be made for the approval of a parent we never had who would speak through our superego, and say, "I love you, you *are* acceptable, you do *not* have to feel guilty"—instead of the superego we do have which says, "You *are* guilty, you do *not* deserve to be loved," and so on. We seem to be built with this longing or home-sickness for an accepting parent who says to us in a way we can really grasp, "You are a fine person, you've done an O.K. job. I really love you even though you aren't perfect." And if we do not have some of this affirmation in the midst of our "inner family" struggle, we may find ourselves bogged down with feelings of restless, lonely incompleteness—as so many people are today.

An individual's background and the strength of his physiological drives generally determine whether Id, Ego, or Superego will dominate the brothers' battles. In the man with apparently no morals,[1] Id reigns supreme with the help of a clever ego. But in the rigid legalistic Christian's life, Superego demands adherence to gain hoped-for approval. And he forces Ego to put the clamps on even natural and healthy need satisfactions which we have been trained to believe are "not nice." But Id is so strong and his needs so demanding that a legalistically pure Christian sometimes finds himself "sinning against his will" (as Paul did) on "sudden impulse from out of the blue." And later he is bewildered yet whipped with guilt by Superego.

Looking at our little inner family of orphan brothers, we see a certain sadness and sense of defeat. One part of us wants to be a fine person, but another says, "You must get money, power, or influence to survive." And we argue within ourselves in making important decisions, "Shall we do the *fine* thing or the thing which will get us ahead faster?" We are pulled back and forth inside.[2]

In our group of becomers we have been appalled at how many times our decisions are influenced in the direction of self-glorification—when we had consciously rationalized them to be "for God" or other people. We found a great need to have our decisions "look right" to

1. Sometimes called a "sociopath."
2. Theoretically I realize this is a loose usage of Freud's notions about the id. The material represented by id's action in personality conflict is repressed material and thus *unconscious*. But I am here referring to id's function in reducing tension under the pleasure principle. The purpose of these chapters is to introduce a simple and necessarily distorted line-drawing of Freud's complex intellectual masterpiece.

ourselves. Because when we are not perfect, "little brother" condemns us by saying things like, "Look, you *are guilty*, you thought or acted *wrongly.* You are *rejected!*" We protect ourselves from this punishment by trying to avoid being wrong or admitting it (since if we can convince ourselves that we aren't wrong, we think we won't have to feel guilty). Sometimes I will do almost anything to avoid admitting I'm wrong, because to admit that would be to agree with the superego's apparent assessment that I am no good anyway (since I can't seem to do right). So I catch myself denying all signs of being wrong. I try to look bright, adequate, honorable, and to wear clothes or accomplish tasks or appear in that light which will make me look "not wrong."

Further, in our society, part of the unexamined folklore makes people think that *failure* is closely linked with being unrighteous or wrong. So we also avoid *failure* as much as we do admitting we're wrong. We do this by working compulsively and by hiding our failures from the world. But this secretiveness only accentuates our *inner* sense of loneliness, inadequacy, and guilt.

It is no wonder that our conscious life, represented by Ego, has a sense of lonely, anxious separation and unacceptableness. And since Id and Superego operate mostly in the unconscious part of our experience, we are often baffled concerning the source of the conflict and guilt which seem to appear out of nowhere.

In summary, the inner condition caused by the lack of total conflict resolution "feels like" an overall need for acceptance, love, and forgiveness of the whole family "just as it is" with all its different strivings. And this state of need is amazingly close to the biblical view of man without God.

Purpose of Superego: Judge? Or Messenger from God?

But wait. There is something else about the activities of the superego. It's not just the distorted "resident representative" of our parents and their moral values.[3] The superego is a built-in mechanism which keeps pushing us *beyond* the animal drives and *beyond* the ego's "enlightened self-interest," demanding that we do the "right" thing—whatever the cost. It is the superego which *stops us in our headlong plunge into total self-centeredness!* It seems to me that the superego's implicit "purpose" is to try to keep us from settling for anything less than a goal which is beyond our inner resources: moral *perfection.* In other words, this part of our personality seems to *expect* and *demand* a kind of perfection or wholeness our animal nature cannot envision. And it is the "little brother" which keeps us searching for something outside ourselves which will still the restless longing we feel to be rightly related to the Truth and yet to our own human natures.

But as a receptacle for the spirit and values of our imperfect parents, the superego cannot meet its needs to be in touch with the truth. And without forgiveness for its imperfect record, it cannot experience the love it makes us yearn for. And so the longing among men everywhere becomes an aching for a Perfect Parent who can give us both the love our inner separation cries out for and the forgiveness and inner reconciliation our human parents could not give. Because this longing for a caring perfect parent figure is almost universal, Freud assumed

---

3. That is, our parents and society *as we understood them when we were about five years old.* And when they "speak to us" now through our superegos, we often experience the *same* guilty *feelings* we had as children.

that man had invented such a Father and called him "God." But since other human hungers have actual satisfiers in man's experience, and since human fathers do not in fact satisfy these deepest needs, it seems just as reasonable an hypothesis to assume that the universal hunger and need for a father-like God exist *because there really is one to meet those needs.*

And the test of whether or not God is a projection of man's imagination or is real would come through accepting him as one who can love us, forgive us, and meet our need to be in touch with truth. If the results of such an experiment over a long period of time tended toward freedom from neurotic guilt and restlessness, toward creativity and loving concern for other people, and an inner reconciliation of forces within our lives, one would at least have to conclude that the Christian God behaves differently (and in fact in the opposite direction) from any other "projection" in the ego's arsenal.

What I believe to be true is that implanted in man's three-sided make-up is a need for reconciliation and a kind of love and forgiveness which only God can give him. If this is true, the superego could be the receptacle built into the human personality for the resident (Holy) Spirit of that transcendent Father—to mediate his love and values to each of us personally.

Without God's presence the superego is programed for moralistic rules with no tolerance for errors (like the Old Testament laws). But with the forgiveness of God's Spirit, the superego could contain a guide with a creative loving perspective, pointing us to greater fulfillment than animal comforts and liberating us to risk without so much terror, since we can be forgiven and begin again ... and again. And we are built to settle for nothing less.

As Augustine said it: We are made for you, God, and "our hearts are restless until they find their rest in Thee."

Some Conclusions about the Freudian Model

If I don't understand the very natural inner warfare or have some picture of the forces struggling within me, I may feel alienated and bewildered and not understand my behavior. When I used to strike out at my wife just when I wanted most to be loved, I thought it was because she was making me feel unworthy—since I didn't consciously see any reason in *my own* behavior for feeling unworthy. But now I realize that the real source of my guilt may be my overactive superego, not my wife.[4]

At times when I feel guilty after doing something *I* do not *consciously* think is wrong, I can see that it may be because my father thought such behavior was wrong and fed that into my superego. I remember talking with a man who felt terribly guilty after going to a movie on Sunday, even though he did not believe going to movies on Sunday was wrong (and the movie was a Christian story). During our conversation he remembered that his mother had thought going to movies on Sunday was a *terrible* sin—and he had "forgotten" or repressed the fact that she felt that way—but his superego had not.

My own anxiety about the future when my prospects are brightest may be just another example of my strict superego scaring me by making me feel unworthy of love—and therefore of success. So I sometimes get the uneasy feeling that things are bound to go wrong— whether or not there is any *evidence* in my real situation.

My irrational need for approval by influential and

---

4. Of course, sometimes it could be one's wife.

successful people is a part of the same deep need to be loved by a powerful parent, and the fear that I will not be. The strong need to succeed in ventures I don't care about and to complete them at any cost has to do with pleasing my superego programed by my mother, who always said, "Be a good boy and finish your spinach." And when I finished it, I got a kiss. So the programed "little brother" counts on me to finish things whether or not it's realistic or wise to do so—or he will make me suffer with guilt and feelings of being unloved.

This is *not* an attempt to blame *parents* and their past teaching for our behavior. As Christians, I believe we must take responsibility for our own actions. And I am convinced that non-neurotic discipline and tenacity are *good* traits. But often we blame those *around us now* when the source of our distress and guilt is *within our inner lives and past histories*. Most parents seem to do the best they can, given their limitations. The amazing news of the gospel is that God can handle and heal even the apparently irreparable past.

The baffling inner conflict goes on between these three forces in our lives as we try to meet our immediate living requirements and search the world over to satisfy our long-range needs for inner security, love, and esteem.

Twelve

The Course of Life: a Hierarchy of Needs

W HEN I was first wrestling with the way our inner needs affect our ability to receive the gospel, I noticed a strange phenomenon. One time after I had spoken to an adult class which I'd been teaching for some months, a man came up and said, "Good lesson! I think that was the first time I really *heard* the gospel," and he actually seemed to mean what he said. But a few seconds later someone else in the *same* group commented (with at *least* equal sincerity), "Well, you've taught some good ones, but *that* one really *missed*. It just didn't *sound like* the gospel! Besides, people aren't interested in the problems you talked about anymore."

When these kinds of contradicting responses to the same communication first began to appear, I thought it was because people had very different intellectual conceptions about what the gospel is (and that's partially true). But after fifteen years of trying to communicate to all different sorts of denominational and nondenominational groups, I have become convinced that in a majority of cases the *differences* in *response* had to do with *different levels of need in the lives of the listeners.*

If this were true, then I realized how important it would be to know the way our needs develop and change, and how these changing needs might affect our perception of life and the Christian faith.

Maslow's Approach

A few years ago a psychologist named Abraham Maslow decided that if we want to find out what people with their basic needs should be like when they are *most whole,* we should study the *healthiest, most adequate* men and women we can find—people who seem to be most nearly fulfilling their inherent potential.[1]

In 1954 Maslow came out with a theory of human motivation[2] which makes a great deal of sense to me and helps explain the way our "ears" as well as our behaviors are affected by the dominant needs which absorb our lives at any given time.

Maslow's picture is only one model and it is not by any means complete. But it has been invaluable to me in beginning to understand more about why people respond or fail to respond to certain presentations of the

----

1. This movement came to be called "the 3rd force in psychology" or the "human potential movement" and includes a growing body of "humanistic" psychologists who are neither Freudians nor behaviorists in their approach to the study of human behavior.

2. See *Motivation and Human Behavior*, rev. ed. (New York: Harper & Row, 1970).

gospel. I want to sketch briefly here one account of the way man's basic needs develop and affect his life, including his belief. For Maslow (1970) man is inherently good. His basic inner direction is toward wholeness or fulfilling his inherent potential—as an acorn seems to "strive" toward becoming an oak tree. This tendency toward self-realization is called "self-actualization." [3] But the overall tendency toward self-realization in man is weaker than his more basic needs and is easily squelched. We sacrifice our higher dreams and potentials in order to meet our more pressing survival needs. And the social pressures we encounter while trying to meet our more urgent needs often stifle our hopes of self-actualization.

A "Hierarchy of Needs"

Maslow felt that a person begins life with a dominant set of overall needs which motivate his behavior and shape his thinking. Until these basic necessities are provided in a reliable and continuing manner, which the person can project into the future, his life will be dominated by them. And he will not be deeply interested in other things while this domination lasts.

But when this first cluster of needs has been regularly and dependably met, Maslow felt that a new and "higher" set of dominant requirements would take over the motivat-

---

3. For Maslow's (1970) description of the "hierarchy of needs" see *Motivation and Personality*, p. 35–58. The description presented in the present book was adapted freely from the books and articles credited to Maslow in the bibliography. Because of obvious space limitations in a book of this nature, I have not dealt extensively with objections and criticisms of Maslow's ideas. My purpose here is only to indicate the developmental nature and direction of man's changing needs.

ing center of one's life—reshaping his current desires, behaviors, and perception, as he sets out to meet the *new* cluster of needs. In this way a person develops through a "hierarchy of needs" from the basic animal-survival necessities to the "higher" more *uniquely human and spiritual needs*. And the meeting of these succeeding clusters of dominant needs constitutes everyone's primary psychological task in life.

Physiological Needs

Now imagine that as a child the first group of needs you had were what Maslow called *Physiological Needs*— the needs for food, oxygen, temperature regulation, thirst satisfaction, rest, sex, elimination, and so on. When these are dominant in a child (or in a primitive people), then the way he spends his time, his planning for the future, and his relating to people are all shaped and largely determined by efforts to get his physiological needs met. And a person's philosophical and theological concerns are deeply, though unconsciously, affected by his dominant needs.

What for instance would "heaven" or total fulfillment look like to a person in the physiological need state? It would likely be a "banquet table" or a place where one would have physiological comfort and completion, perhaps with plenty of sexual fulfillment. And when one looks at primitive religions of people in the physiological need stage, these are often their images of heaven or ultimate fulfillment. Therefore, someone preaching a gospel of salvation which had nothing to say about physiological needs would most likely *not be relevant* to a child (or a people) in that need stage.[4]

---

4. Maslow was not a Christian and did not deal with the

Safety Needs

But if a person (or people) has his physiological needs met in a dependable and recurring fashion, then, although he will still have physiological requirements all his life, they will move off the *center* stage of his attention into the background, and a new cluster of dominant needs will occupy his primary attention and color his motivated behavior and thought life. As each dominant group of needs is replaced, it does not cease to be active. For instance, the memory of hunger as a child may continue to motivate a wealthy adult. But the more primitive necessities usually become less consciously demanding, since one is no longer "afraid" that they will never be provided.[5]

Maslow called this second constellation of needs the *Safety Needs*, which include needs for physical safety, shelter, economic security, psychological safety, emotional surety, and preference for the familiar (see picture of Hierarchy of Needs: figure 3, p. 94).

A little boy may be terribly afraid of the dark, but as his overall safety becomes assured, he should develop through this stage. But a person who never had his safety

---

relevance of this theory for Christian communication. These interpretations were made after a careful study of Maslow's model.

5. It is also true that there may be overlapping and reversals in any given life history with regard to the dominance of a particular need cluster. For example, it has been shown that babies in what would normally be considered the physiological need state can die from lack of love and affection. Also in certain cases the need for esteem is so great that men would go without food or water to maintain their self-respect. Usually in actual experience any single act may be motivated by a combination of several needs. But generally, the developmental course described by Maslow would seem to be true to the experience of most people.

needs met dependably may go on developing physically, but all his life he may be in some ways stuck at the safety need stage. He may appear to be strong and confident but have fears regarding his safety which seem irrational for a grown man. Such a person, whose dominant need is for security, may have to return and check the back door several times before he is sure he locked it.[6] He may fear constantly for his health. Or as an adult, he may become convinced that "every long-haired kid is a Communist" and begin to fill his basement with

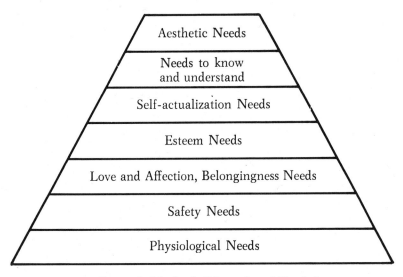

Figure 3. Maslow's Hierarchy of Needs [7]

6. Although this rather common obsession may relate to many other causes (see Freud, 1960).
7. Many pictures of Maslow's hierarchy stop at Self-actualization needs. In his 1970 revision he included the needs to "know and understand" and the "aesthetic needs" as higher needs states after discovering many people are motivated by them as a part of self-actualization.

guns to protect what he has. Impulses toward safety and
self-preservation are natural, but when the security needs
are dominant and basically unsatisfied, they can lead to
an oppressive and fearful way of life.
This cluster of needs would also affect one's philosophical and theological concerns. What for instance would
ultimate fulfillment or "heaven" look like to a man in the
security need stage? It would probably be a place where
he was eternally "safe" from harm or at least from evil,
death, and hell. So in order to be relevant for people in
this stage, the preacher would have to concentrate on the
security aspect of the grace of God in Christ, the *saving*
of men from death and hell. And a man in this stage who
heard a sermon about heaven as a banquet table or a place
where sex needs were met would probably consider the
sermon naïve and largely irrelevant, since his own life is
focused on finding and maintaining security. If the sermon
doesn't describe the fear of hell and the safety of salvation,
it simply "does not sound like the gospel." [8]

Belongingness or Love Needs

But if and when the *Safety* requirements have been
put to rest as the dominant ones, then the *Love* and
Affection or *Belongingness Needs* tend to take over as
the all-absorbing focus in a person's life. When a child
is getting enough to eat and feels safe in his world, he

---

8. I am not saying that a preacher should *bend* the gospel to
fit man's various needs. There is an assumption behind this presen-
tation that God has made it *his business* to help men deal with
their own most basic needs, and that the gospel announces this
(Matt. 6:25–34). Besides, it seems reasonably certain to me that
any message not relevant to dominant needs will not be taken too
seriously in any case in terms of eliciting deeply motivated behavior.

begins to relate to other people in a different way. He
wants to be loved, have feelings of acceptance and belonging, companionship and friendship, affection and
love—both giving and receiving. And these needs are
dramatically apparent among young people today, particularly teen-agers. Because so many of them have had
their basic physiological and security needs met through
their parents' efforts, they are crying out, "Love is all that
matters." "Love" is written across their sweatshirts and
across their conscious minds as the focus and goal of
life. Young girls are hitchhiking alone across America in
search of love, not concerned with their safety—in spite
of the fact that hardly a week goes by when the news-
papers don't report some young girl having been raped
or murdered on the highways.

And what would "heaven" look like to a person in the
belongingness and love need stage? It would probably be
a place or state of being in which one feels that God
loves him and *accepts* him *just as he is*—where all people love each other and love is the purpose and end of
life. Such a person would probably think sermons on
"God's provision" of physiological needs or "saving from
hellfire and damnation" were unsophisticated and out-
dated.

5 1

Esteem Needs

After *Love* and *Belongingness* come the *Esteem Needs:*
the search for self-respect, the esteem and respect of
others, status, prestige, recognition, importance, approval
—independence of personality leading to feelings of self-
confidence, adequacy, of being of use, and having worth.[9]

9. It is interesting to note that a large part of the "Jesus movement" is tying into the needs for structure and security *as well as*

These needs often determine people's vocational direction if they are central at the time one is choosing a vocation. To meet one's needs in this area, the esteem received must be genuine. If it is feigned, the person seeking it will likely be frustrated and forced into neurotic posturing—unconsciously acting (somehow unconvincingly) as if he *has* the esteem which he is afraid at a deep level he does *not* have or deserve.

This happened to me. As a young boy, I felt my father valued and loved my older brother more than me. My mother gave me almost unconditional love and attention. She was so constantly affirming that I couldn't *believe* her love. I just knew I didn't deserve it. I began to shape my life to get my father's esteem. He was a rather undemonstrative man. And through my own experience I learned a real truth about the way people's lives are shaped by their attempts to get their esteem needs met.

In order to get my father's attention I began to respond with behavior I knew he would approve. I majored in business and finance in college because I knew that is what dad wanted me to do—even though I was much more interested in subjects like communication, English, history, and theology. I was the kind of kid who read Shakespeare behind *Playboy,* instead of the other way around. 54:30 57

Outwardly life seemed to be progressing normally and rapidly, but inwardly I was very unhappy. And when someone came close to revealing my true self to me (or challenged my inflated masculine identity), I was furious. But not being able to face revealing my phoniness, I

---

the love and affection needs, which could give it great appeal to a group having sought security and love in a good many self-defeating ways.

would wait and "get back" at them at another point in our relationship. For instance, early in our marriage if my wife might imply that she would rather continue reading *Better Homes and Gardens* than make love on a given evening, I would be furious. But instead of facing my masculine pride and insecurity directly, I'd wait a couple of days until she did some little thing like burn the toast at breakfast. Then I would explode and (emotionally) throw the plateful of toast across the room. She would be amazed and feel that my behavior was a little strong for "toast." And it was, but she did not know that the *real* offense occurred two days before. So I became a phony person fighting my battles on the wrong battlefields.

As a counselor, I have talked to teen-age girls who desperately needed a feeling of belonging and of being loved and who had traded their bodies to have these needs for acceptance met. I have listened to boys who are becoming something they do not want to be, hoping to find a shortcut to having their esteem needs met. I know women who have married the wrong men because of the tremendous pressure our society puts on them to be married by the age of twenty-five.

In communicating the good news of Jesus Christ it has been very valuable to me to realize how many *millions* of people today are living unreal lives. And yet it's clear that many of them are secretly looking for a way to become themselves and yet meet their needs for self-esteem. But it is also true that thousands *in the church* have given up and are living behind facades which were formed to implement the meeting of needs for security, love, and esteem.

What would heaven or ultimate fulfillment look like

to a person enmeshed in meeting the *Esteem* needs? It would probably be a place where one would feel a great sense of worth, of being highly valued by God and other people—not because of vastly superior performance or possessions but simply for himself. A Christian witness who only talked about "hellfire" would miss such a person almost totally. Whereas a speaker who emphasized the point that "because God loves you, you *are* somebody" might hit the listener right in the heart. I believe some of the most outstanding preachers in minority groups today are realizing this. And they are beginning to relate the gospel to newly surfacing needs for esteem in their people's lives.

But if and when the *Esteem* needs have been dependably met, there comes a cluster of needs Maslow felt were so unusual as to be almost of a different order from those described so far.[10]

---

10. According to Harlow, apes evidently have physiological, belongingness, and even esteem needs.

Thirteen

Breaking Through
Toward Liberation

AFTER a person has had his basic *Physiological,*
Safety, Love, and *Esteem* requirements met, he may enter
the stage of the *Self-Actualization* needs. These include
the desire for creativity and self-expression, the need for
realizing one's highest potential, for mature relationships
with others, for religious and artistic expression, and for
feelings of growth. What appears to happen at this point
is that an individual has enough of his basic needs met to
risk letting down his mask of unreality, which seemed necessary for security and affirmation before. And as one
lets down the conscious and unconscious facades, he begins to get in touch with his real self with its often buried
hopes and dreams.

During this process he may have startling experiences
through which freeing insights and self-revelations occur.

These experiences, which Maslow called *peak-experiences*, are very positive, very meaningful, and often result in life-long changes of perception. Such an experience may occur once or many times, but each peak-experience seems to be an enhancing, horizon-expanding encounter with reality.

A person at this stage may change vocations, change his life-style, take up new hobbies and relationships, and begin to lead a new and expanded existence. He is less afraid of the unknown and capable of much deeper interpersonal relations. It has been said that the onset of the self-actualization needs is almost like being "born again." But in Maslow's studies of life histories he said that people who reach the stage of "self-actualization" are as rare as Olympic gold medal winners in the total population of athletes. And as I recall, he did not find a single case of a self-actualizer under *fifty years old.*

What then might "heaven" or ultimate fulfillment look like to a person struggling to meet his self-actualization needs? It might be a state in which he is free to be himself and to participate in creative activities to which he could give his all with abandon. And, in hearing the Christian message, unless such a person heard something of "God's gift of freedom and of man's being made to be creative in the image of God," he might consider the gospel irrelevant to his basic concerns.

It is interesting to note that these self-actualizers had a great sensitivity to pain and suffering. And they were able to risk and relate much less defensively and more personally than other people. Maslow also said that such persons have a "God-like quality" in their freedom and wisdom about life.

Needs to Know and Understand

When an individual begins to get in touch with himself and with the freedom to develop his true potential, a new group of motivating needs or desires may become apparent: those clustering around *the desire to Know and Understand*. Some of the characteristics of this stage are: an increased curiosity, the desire for unification of collected concepts and bits of philosophy, and an integration of religious beliefs in relation to the world. In other words, after the awesome realization that he is free to *become* what he truly *is*, a man or woman may develop a need to relate this becoming self to a larger view of life and the world in order to approach a deeper and more total integration.

"Heaven" in this stage might appear to be a place where people study, think about great questions, and examine theories concerning their solutions.

Most of the professors I've met who teach in theological seminaries appear to be motivated by the needs to *know* and *understand*—even if they have by-passed the resolution of security, love, esteem, or self-actualization stages. Such men often teach seminarians to deal with theological issues and problems from the perspective of the needs to know and understand. The horrible fallacy involved in this approach is that most of the future ministers' *congregations* will be absorbed with the *very different* perspectives involved in the needs for security, love, and esteem. So in seminaries where this situation may exist, students are unknowingly *being trained* in a perspective which will be psychologically irrelevant to most of their parishioners.[1]

_____

1. Ideally the seminarian needs to be exposed to the most pro-

Aesthetic Needs

Finally Maslow described a group of needs for the person who had found himself and gotten his intellectual world together: the *Aesthetic Needs*. At this point man has a craving for beauty, symmetry, order, harmony, a desire for perfection of structure and form, ecstasy and mystic experience. In other words, at this state of being a person moves into the immediacy of experience. He does not love the truth and beauty for what they can *do* for him in trying to accomplish other goals. He loves the truth simply because *it is* true and the beautiful because of the joy of experiencing it.[2]

Such a person would obviously have a very different set of goals and behaviors from someone dominated by the *Physiological* or *Safety* needs, for instance. And what might heaven look like in this perspective? It might well be a state in which a man or woman knew God directly and personally and would simply enjoy him forever. And of course a minister who preached the gospel to a congregation of people in the *Aesthetic* need stage (if indeed one existed) would very likely miss them with a "hellfire and damnation" sermon which did not even touch on the joyous "friendship" with God through Christ.

Relation of Denominations to Need States

After considering Maslow's model in the light of the

---

found knowledge and understanding his professors can muster. But unless the student can relate his knowledge and understanding to the dominant needs of his parishioners, they may never hear him. The only solution I can see is for seminary faculties and students to move toward being communities of fellow-becomers themselves.

2. This need state is in some way amazingly similar to descriptions of Christian saints who love God not for what he can do for them—but simply because he is God.

Christian church's experience, I have come to believe that denominational groups, or more accurately, sub-groups—with their particular emphases—are clustered around different psychological need states. Thus, certain fundamentalist groups appear to be grounded in the *Physiological* and *Security* needs. And when one does not communicate the gospel in terms of "salvation from hell" or "making provision for one's daily bread," some of the members don't feel the gospel has been preached.

But other groups have been attracted to Christ when they bogged down in their attempts to meet their *Love and Belongingness* needs. And to such groups, the gospel hasn't been preached unless the communication thrust is toward God's amazing love and acceptance of us and our opportunity to love other people by meeting their needs. There might be a strong tendency toward meeting in small groups to learn to give and receive love. And as I have suggested, a person in this sort of setting might think a congregation in which the gospel was couched in terms of "hellfire and damnation" was irrelevant and naïve. In fact such Christians might bore him.

Of course the same kinds of distinctions might be applicable to a group whose entrance into the Kingdom was related to their *Esteem, Self-Realization, Knowing,* or *Aesthetic* needs. The difference being that the further up the hierarchy of needs one goes, the more overlapping of stages he may expect. This is because the satisfiers for the higher needs are a good bit more varied than for the lower ones. A man who is hungry can only be satisfied by food. And he can often not think of ultimate fulfillment or wholeness apart from being fed. But a man who needs esteem can get it from many different sources—from the crowd's applause, on one hand, to a solitary response concerning a scholarly article, on the other. So, in those denominations clustering around the "higher" needs on Maslow's scale, one would expect a good bit more tolerance for variety in the communication of the gospel.[3] And in fact this seems to be true.

In actual practice, of course, most denominations have pockets of people in many of the need stages described. But the dominant "position" of many denominations or sub-groups seems to fit the picture given. Since so many children "inherit" their denominational affiliation, they often find, upon growing up and learning the church's basic stance, that it has little to say to their own dominant needs. Many people today, who have been converted as adults, have changed denominations in order to find a church where the "true gospel is preached," often meaning: where the gospel which first *"spoke to my condition"* is preached. And members of the old denomination are hurt and bewildered—since their church *evidently* preaches about the same redeeming Lord as the new church.

So a preacher might find it wise to vary his sermons in such a way as to show how God speaks to man in different stages of need if he plans to reach his whole congregation over a year's time.[4]

---

3. For the Christian, of course, one need stage is no better or more prestigious than another. And in this regard it is unfortunate that Maslow used the terms "higher" and "lower." In fact, the lack of faith and commitment in those bodies formed around the so-called higher need stages may outweigh much of the alleged tolerance.

4. One reason for the success of the lay witness movement in motivating different kinds of people is that a *number* of speakers witness to the *point of need* at which God met them. And their experiences represent a spectrum of needs on Maslow's Hierarchy

The point of this is that there seems to be definite correlation between an individual's motivational need stage and that of the person or group which is most likely to lead him to a Christian conversion. And his theology will be shaped at least as much by his psychological needs as by historical considerations. Each group seems to select those emphases from the Bible and tradition which substantiate its experience of God's redeeming activity—and to repress those elements which don't. And if God in fact speaks to the whole of man's pilgrimage, each group can prove that *its* approach is scriptural.

Maslow's Theories and Christian Conversion

But how does Christian development plug into a picture of motivation like Maslow's? I checked the psychological Abstracts from their beginning to Maslow's work. And although I did not find a Christian motivational model, the *experience* of "Christian conversion" seemed very similar in some ways to Maslow's "peak-experiences" in the lives of self-actualizers.

As I studied dozens of accounts of conversions in the lives of outstanding men and women, I began to believe the hypothesis implied in the previous paragraphs: that there may be a real correlation between what happens to a person through becoming a Christian and the meeting of different clusters of needs in Maslow's hierarchy. And I saw some interesting comparisons.

For instance, none of Maslow's subjects evidently waded through the physiological, safety, love, and esteem

---

with which listeners can identify—and which no single pastor's experiences could encompass.

stages to become a self-actualizer until he was fifty years old. Yet some great Christians were converted and displayed a number of self-actualizer characteristics years earlier in their lives (for example, Augustine, Luther, Wesley).[5]

What may have happened is that through a significant conversion experience some Christians have had *several* of their basic clusters of needs met by God and the church. For instance, through a deep realization that he is loved and accepted unconditionally by God and his people, a person could feel that he is *safe* in the world. He could realize that he is *loved* and has a family to which he belongs in the church. And at the same time the new Christian could grasp the fact that he is *esteemed* not because of his accomplishments but because he is unconditionally accepted by One of ultimate importance— God. If this is a true hypothesis, then it will be possible to account for the fact that self-actualizing behavior could take place earlier in a deeply converted Christian than in one who had to battle every step (or rung) of the way up the hierarchy of needs. And it would mean

---

5. Although some critics have implied that one or all of these men became narrow religious fanatics, a closer look seems to reveal something quite different in terms of psychological dynamics. Particularly in the cases of Luther and Wesley, their conversions from a tight, rigid, miserable introspection and self-centeredness led them to create almost a new style of life for the believers of their time. When one thinks of the courage necessary for an Augustinian monk, or an Anglican parson to stand alone and say that the *entire religious world from whence he came* was mistaken, such a change is certainly significant. And since in each case the change was toward a deeper relatedness to people and a wider more vulnerable style of living and loving, emotional wholeness rather than illness seems to be indicated. Incidentally Maslow found that each self-actualizer had certain marked exceptions to his generally free and creative behavior. None was perfect.

that God has given us a way to be liberated from the uncreative tyranny of our more primitive motivational pressures.[6]

I realize that a conscientious theologian may object that I am defining the gospel in terms of man's needs. But I am *not* trying to be a theologian in this discussion. I am talking about needs man *actually experiences* throughout his life. And I believe that a personal relationship with God and his people can sometimes provide the security, love, esteem, etc. which man must find in order to meet his most basic needs and accomplish his psychological life's work.

But it is obvious to anyone who is around the church these days that *very few* Christians are displaying self-actualizing behavior.[7] As I began to read more about the lives of Christians who have evidenced the creative freedom Maslow described, I saw that most of them had come down an amazingly similar *trail of inner events* which led to some kind of "conversion experience."

I became very excited about studying the conversion experience. If I am going to spend my life trying to com-

---

6. It is important to remember that each need in the hierarchy continues to exist for each person throughout his life—even if it ceases to be the dominant motivating force.

7. After conversion, when a new Christian has the particular cluster of needs met which originally drove him to turn to God, he sometimes thinks he has "outgrown" Christianity—since he's no longer haunted by the needs which seemed so tied up with his conversion to Christ. And he becomes disinterested. But according to the view I am proposing, God and the gospel are creatively relevant to *each* new stage of man's motivational development throughout his life. If this is true, the effective preacher's communication job is at least partially to interpret the gospel's relevance to the *crises* and *changes* which people experience as they move *beyond* the needs which brought them to Christ toward *new* clusters of needs, insecurities, and temptations.

municate the gospel of Jesus Christ, I would like to do it in a way that might lead to profound changes in people's lives. To do this I have often felt the need for some kind of picture or model to study. This model should describe the steps or stages a person might go through from a rank pagan beginning to a conversion experience which frees him to become the creative person he was "designed" to be.

Numerous studies have shown that when a doctor or psychologist (or for that matter almost anyone trying to help solve problems) can anticipate the course of diseases or events, his success in dealing with the difficulties involved improves tremendously. "Anticipatory information," writes psychologist Hugh Bowen, "allows . . . a dramatic change in performance."

Question III

What Happens in Conversion?

Introduction

THE research on which the following chapters are based indicates that there are distinct traditions for both "gradual" and "sudden" conversions to Christianity (see William James, 1902, p. 186f.). For some people conversion may seem to be sudden, like walking down the street, having the street break open, and falling through. For others the experience appears to be gradual. This gradual sort has been compared to the course of a sunflower as it turns imperceptibly toward the sun, but in the end is facing it.

But since all the accounts of Christian conversions which I read included the more dramatic life-changing type of experience, the following model will reflect that study.[1] And in the rest of this book I shall mean by the term *conversion:* that identifiable experience through which a person becomes unified and consciously in right relationship with God, other people, and the world. The experience is accompanied by or closely associated with an act of personal "turning loose" or commitment to God, as he is revealed in Jesus Christ. This beginning

1. This is not dismissing gradual types of Christian change as valid. But the questions giving rise to this section concerned the more identifiable conversion experience.

results in a permanent reorientation toward God and toward trying to live the caring, vulnerable, and liberated life-style seen in Jesus Christ.

I have come to believe that a *genuinely transforming conversion experience* is historically a relatively *rare thing* even among Christians. Therefore, the following picture may not relate to the experience of many people. But the effects of such deeply converted lives have been disproportionate with regard to their number in the church. So an attempt to reconstruct a modern inner map of the terrain and paths leading to conversion seems at least worth trying.

I shall draw a composite sketch from autobiographies, biographies, personal experiences, historical and other literary sources, and interviews with creative people who have reported Christian conversions in their own lives. This will be an "outline of a pilgrimage" toward being converted in the more dramatic or "sudden" way. There will of course be overlapping and reversals when compared to any specific life. And there may be omissions of certain "stages" in the life of any particular person heading toward conversion. But such oversimplification is apparently unavoidable in presenting models of an aspect of life which is dynamic and personal.

Fourteen

Man's Condition on His Own

MAN'S condition, according to Christian tradition, is that he was created to be basically *good*, happy, and loving. We were made in the image of God (Gen. 1)—to be related to him. But in every case this image has been blurred. It seems that although we were originally designed to be free and loving, each of us chooses instead to spend his energies in various compulsive attempts to *be* God in our relationships to him, to other people, and to the material objects around us. We try to be the "most important one" and to control people around us in different ways. As the late Archbishop William Temple (1963, p. 24) said, ". . . there is only one sin, and it is characteristic of the whole world. It is the self-will which prefers 'my' way to God's—which puts 'me' in the center where only God is in place." As we do this, we become lonely pilgrims without knowing how it happened, somehow alienated from our given potential by a separation which extends to the core of our being. This *separation*, which Christianity says has been here since the first man, is called "sin."

The practical problem with trying to *be* God in one's own little world is that evidently no man can command the sort of universal approval and success the "role of God" calls for. It's an insatiable need. And regardless of the *size* of our achievements, we are left with a strange, lonely incompleteness or a sense that there has to be "more to life than this."

Paul Tillich (1949, p. 151) said that the state of our whole life is estrangement from others and ourselves—because we are estranged from the origin and aim of our lives. We do not know where we have come from or where we are going. So we try to create a controllable "game plan." We do this so we can repress our deep sense of separation. For if we think about it, we become terrified by such specters as the ultimate void of our own death and nothingness.

There are several basic problems like this which are so universal they appear to be built into man's mind. And even if we repress these questions, we seem to set out unconsciously to provide answers for ourselves. Or we try to structure our own little worlds in such a way that the queries never come up. Some of these questions are:[1] Is reality evil and pushing toward death, or good and pressing toward hope? Does life have any meaning and purpose or is it a meaningless "tale told by an idiot"? What is the nature of the Really Real? And finally and most importantly, will everything come out all right in the end for me? Will life triumph over death somehow, or will death wear the grim (and only) smile at the end of

1. See Andrew Greeley (1971).

the play? The frantic rush of all our efforts seems to imply a fear that things will not come out all right in the end. So we hurry and build our kingdoms before we are defeated by death.

But I am getting ahead of my story. The point is that our "sensing," however vaguely, that life can be more than it is, sets up a tension inside us as we deal with the real world. This tension, aided by our superego, won't let us stop when our achievements have secured us enough to eat and drink. The intuitive feeling that we have a destiny beyond our present accomplishments provides the conscious motivating force which drives us toward ever greater goals.

Many people say that such a feeling of separation and tension is unhealthy. But as Viktor Frankl (1964, p. 163) has pointed out, this tension is an indispensable prerequisite of mental health. That is, it motivates people not to settle for physical comforts but to seek a more whole and complete condition. We are, it seems, on an unconscious search for liberation and wholeness.

A strange feature of this struggle is that each of us evidently feels that his own basic tenseness and anxiety about the incompleteness of life is somehow unique. However, as psychologist George Kisker (1964) says, this condition of anxious unsettledness is true for almost everybody most of the time.

But the average person will probably *not* see the source of his deep lack of satisfaction as resulting from a separation from God. We more often interpret our restlessness as due to our *lack of achievement* or our inability to get control of our environment. We cannot manipulate the people around us completely enough to have them fulfill our needs for physiological goodies, security, affirmation,

and esteem—which will, we feel, be met through achievements, conquests, and acquisitions of various kinds. When
we are young, our "progress" may be fast enough that
we can avoid or repress conscious anxiety—believing we
will continue to succeed through what appears to be an
endless sea of time ahead of us.

During all this striving and achieving we may have no
consciousness of God. But since the Christian belief is
that man's basic problem is *not* lack of achievement in
his external environment, we are doomed to frustration.
Besides, Christians believe that our strong bent toward
glorifying ourselves will make us foul our own inner
nest—even when we have succeeded magnificently in
manipulating our environment.

Paul Tournier (1962, p. 135) describes this inner bent
by saying that man left to himself is lost. Our own efforts,
our own good will and good intentions, our own virtues
cannot banish our "disease." We are aware that even our
most sincere efforts to banish disease bring new evils in
their train. There seems to be a poison within us, given
with life itself and present throughout its duration, which
contaminates almost every experience in advance.

At some point in this confusing pattern of achieving
and fouling our own nests, a person's "search" may take
on a new quality of intensity. This happens when the
image of life and success we have invested with ultimate
importance is threatened with destruction. This may take
place either because we are failing in a way we can't
avoid admitting *or* because we have *reached* our goals
and succeeded. If we had counted on "achievement" to
solve our basic self-alienation and meet our dominant
needs, we may be depressed when success is unmistakable,
but does *not* bring the relatedness and wholeness we

dreamed of. If, on the other hand, our failure is stark and apparently irreversible, the psychological effect may be very similar. In either case we have misread our world. Somehow we bet all our happiness and fulfillment capital on the wrong horse.

But part of our bent toward playing God makes it amazingly difficult to admit even to ourselves that we have been wrong in our important judgments. Many of us also find it hard to ask help from another person with regard to our own personal problems. So when the time comes that we must *face* our failure or success, several things may happen to us: Because our own efforts or preconceived solutions to the riddle of life have failed to bring happiness, we may for the first time become conscious of the self-defeating nature of our success oriented life-style. And we may become poignantly aware of our need for "outside help." But there is often a desperate internal struggle before this realization becomes conscious. Most of us repress this need for help, even when it is very obvious to the people around us. In our small group several of us saw how much tragedy and pain we could have avoided if we had gone to someone for help sooner.

Thomas Gordon (1955, p. 83) has described this battle against the conscious discovery of the mistaken foundation stones on which one has tried to build his life. He says that there seems to be something in human nature—whether learned and acquired or rooted in the organic make-up of all living organisms—something that predisposes us to defend our world of reality against the threat of change. We seek the type of experience which supports our present stance and reject experiences—even potentially helpful ones—which seem to promise a disturbance of the current direction for our lives.

Because of this great resistance to change, it is usually only when our old personal world is threatened with destruction or meaninglessness that we may be open to taking seriously a radical change in our life's *purpose* and *direction*. Only when we are somehow blocked in this way will we ordinarily consider a "higher" personal power which might make whole that which is separated in us and find that which is lost.

Fifteen

The
Awareness of God:
the Struggle Begins

WHAT apparently happens when our old world is seriously threatened is that a person's search changes from a conscious wish for *specific solutions*—means and material assistance toward the fulfillment of achievement goals—to a search for overall *healing* and *hope* for *himself*. His thoughts change from "how can I get this project finished" to "I'm confused and miserable and need some help from somewhere to get through today." And Christian tradition indicates that we must have this realization of the need for profound change and for help to accomplish it. These are two of the primary conditions which make a person ready for a new vision of life and of God.

But William James (1902, p. 205) said that besides the feeling of present incompleteness or wrongness from which one is now eager to escape, there must be a growing awareness that there may be something "out there" to respond to—which we have been too busy to notice before. And I found in almost every "case history" there was this dawning awareness of something beyond their own minds—whether the person involved had previously experienced close contact with Christianity or not.

The common feeling of being almost irresistably drawn toward a presence or force beyond themselves seems to be the common experience of all kinds of people as they face the awareness of their own limited humanity. John Knox (1970, p. 84) talks about what common meaning the term *God* may have for different kinds of men as they become aware of the possibility of something to which they might relate beyond themselves. "What, for example," he asks, "is the 'obsession' which Gamaliel Bradford describes as a 'keen, enormous, haunting, never-sated thirst for God'? When Francis Thompson tells of his flight from the 'hound of heaven,' *what* is pursuing him? When Bertrand Russell cries out that the 'center of (him) is always and eternally a terrible pain,' a 'searching for something beyond what the world contains,' what is this something? When Augustine said, 'Thou has made us for thyself and we are restless till we rest in thee,' of whom, or to whom, was he speaking? It is obvious from these examples—that the word 'God' may have the most poignant meaning even for one who doubts or denies his objective reality as an actual being or existence. Bertrand Russell—having spoken of 'something transfigured and infinite, the beatific vision, God,' goes on to say, 'I do not find it, I do not think it is to be found, but the love of it is my life.' "

But even as the potential convert feels a yearning or drawing toward something beyond his own life, he begins to sense a strong resistance within himself to responding to this unknown being or power. This again seems to be a part of our desperate need to be king or god of our own personal worlds. We want to be *helped* and *loved* by God, but we fear that he will absorb us or we will lose our identity and "control" if we get too close to him. We are afraid that he will make us "religious," "unnatural," vulnerable to the ridicule of those whose approval we've always sought. Or as Sören Kierkegaard said, we are afraid that we might live to regret responding to God.

But having tried on our own and realized our human limitations, having faced the inadequacy of our past view of life, and having sensed a calling or yearning toward a person or presence beyond ourselves, we may be almost ready for a Christian conversion.

But before this can happen, it seems that there must be an internal "showdown" leading to a personal crisis of the will. This crisis involves the necessity for us to take a gigantic psychological leap: to acknowledge frankly our sense of worthlessness. Psychologist Hobart Mowrer (1960) in a non-Christian context talks about the necessity and difficulty of honest confession before a new wholeness is possible for a patient in therapy: ". . . we encounter difficulty because human beings do not change radically until they first acknowledge their sins, but it is hard for one to make such an acknowledgment unless he has 'already changed.' In other words, the full realization of deep worthlessness is a severe 'ego insult,' and one must have a new source of strength to endure it." So before we can confess at this depth we usually must have determined at a level unconscious to ourselves that God is real—that he is really "out there."

This difficulty in honestly facing and confessing our helplessness can lead us into an internal struggle which may last for a few hours or for years—until we can envision a new source of strength available to us. Generally the motivation to go on and confess is provided in one of two ways (and often this is where the Christian witness comes in): The struggler may meet a person whose converted life or words about God's loving acceptance and power attract him. This Christian's faith and confidence may reinforce the struggler's yearning *enough* so that he can overcome the fear of surrendering himself (and the god position in his life) to God.

If he does not meet such a Christian, there is another route to the crisis point: The *anxiety* of the struggle may be *heightened* by either circumstances or communication. We may hear in a sermon or begin to suspect that we are *never* going to make it by ourselves. A kind of terror can surface. At that point a frightening confrontation may be precipitated. A genuine religious conversion is evidently the outcome of a crisis. Though this encounter may take place in different circumstances and forms and there may be many preparatory steps, the event of conversion comes to focus in a crisis of ultimate concern. There is in such a conversion a sense of desperate conflict in which one is so involved that his whole meaning and destiny are at stake in a "life or death," all or none significance. Unless a person is aware of a conflict serious enough to defeat him, and unless he is concerned ultimately enough to put his life in the balance, he is not ready for conversion.[1]

So assume that we reach a crisis, confess our self-centeredness and our sense of worthlessness, and really

1. See William James (1902, p. 186f.). Other kinds of crucial change, failure, or tragedy (e.g., divorce, death of a loved one) can precipitate a conversion crisis. But unless the crisis includes the integral elements in the process described here, the resulting conversion may be only a part of the grief reaction. And such "conversions" often evaporate when the crisis is over.

want a new life. Almost all Christian traditions maintain that the next step after confession is *repentance*. But Christian repentance is *not* a mere verbal expression or being "sorry about" certain acts. It is more like an agonizing wrenching as we turn our backs on our own past. It's as if we were pulling our lives up by the roots and replanting them, facing in a different direction. This act of the will constitutes a deep denial of our past direction and becomes a first step toward responding to the God we have sensed was pursuing us.

To summarize the pilgrimage so far: The description of preconversion man pictured a striving person, confident at first that he could find or create the conditions for self-fulfillment on his own. But our attempts to manipulate people and our environment toward material or social success and acclaim finally teach us that we are only human and that our humanity yearns for a kind of relatedness and completion beyond ourselves and our manipulations. We may first experience frustration, then anxiety. And our inner crying out for help, new direction, and meaning may change the focus of our lives from a preoccupation with means to our success-oriented goals to a global need for being saved from the swamp in which our motivational feet are stuck. As this condition approaches consciousness, we may become ready to *confess* our helpless sense of separation and realize that we need to *repent* (or turn from) our past life-style and direction. This sequence may be unconscious until the moment of conversion, or one may be aware of the overall progression described here.

In any case I have found the language difficulties in trying to describe the *actual experience* of conversion to be practically insurmountable.

Sixteen

The Experience of Conversion

IF our basic sin or separation is caused by *inordinate* self-centeredness and worship of ourselves in the place of God, then our hope, according to Christian tradition, lies in restoring God to the center of life. God becomes this center, it seems, when we respond to the love of God as we have discerned it in Jesus Christ.

But the catch is that even if we realize these things, we cannot by our own "insight" recenter our lives. The evidence is overwhelming that most of us simply cannot make this basic change at a purely cognitive level, although many Christian educators seem to have assumed that we can. Carl Jung (1960) said that in the face of the very real powers that dominate us, only an equally real power or encounter can offer help. No intellectual system, but direct experience only, can counterbalance the blind power of our seemingly instinctual course.

The experience of Christian conversion is, in the last

analysis, a solitary one. Preachers, teachers, witnesses, books, and friends can provide information about God and recite inspiring and highly motivating case histories, including their own. But if we are candidates for conversion, we finally reach the point where only we in our aloneness can make a reply—even if there are a thousand people around us at the time. And although it has been described in many ways, this "reply to God" evidently is an attempt at a *specific* and *total commitment* of our future to him.

Many Christian teachers have urged moderation in speaking of the necessity of such a specific commitment, realizing that this more radical conversion is not likely to be the experience of everyone. But Dietrich Bonhoeffer (1960, p. 53) was quite clear in stating the necessity for a definite act at this point. "Unless a definite step is demanded, the call vanishes into thin air; and if men imagine that they can follow Jesus without taking this step they are deluding themselves . . ."

And this act is not merely saying yes to a proposition or creed about God. But as Martin Marty (1962) noted, it means "being grasped." Inside, it is the feeling of *responding*, not of instigating. One feels that *God* is offering the relationship. And this offering on God's part before we have offered, so to speak, is called God's "grace."

Man's specific response has been called in poetic language: "Opening the door (of one's personal life) to Christ." John Stott (1962, p. 130) spells out the difference between this specific opening of one's self and other religious activities when he says that "this step is the beginning and nothing else will do instead. You can believe in Christ intellectually and admire Him; you can say your prayers to Him through the keyhole (as I did for many years)[1]; you can push coins at Him under the door; you can be moral, decent, upright and good; you can be religious and pious; you can have been baptized and confirmed; you can be deeply versed in the philosophy of religion; you can be a theological student and even an ordained minister—and still not have opened the door to Christ. There is no substitute for this."

But here again is the baffling paradox of man seeking—yet running from God, as the moment of conversion is upon him. There must be a resolving of this ambivalence before conversion can be said to have taken place. The potential convert has to feel somehow that he and God are no longer competitors or enemies trying to win a power struggle in the person's life. John Knox (1970, p. 87) helps clarify what is happening in the resolution of this conflict. He reminds us of Alfred North Whitehead's belief that religion runs through three stages if it evolves to its final satisfaction. It is the transition from *God the void* to *God the enemy,* and from *God the enemy* to *God the companion.*

What is meant by *God the companion?* Knox suggests that this stage, when realized (or to the extent it is realized), means a free and inward capitulation to the "enemy," an allowing of ourselves to be captured by the God who seeks us. This stage is the "final satisfaction" because we discover in the moment of surrender that the God who is on our trail is also the God we seek. In a strange manner, as we seem to be defeated, it dawns on us that we are in the only possible way, *victorious!* For we are free from having to run from God (who is everywhere), and we can turn and embrace him.

Our semiconscious fear of surrendering and being to-

---

1. Stott's parentheses.

tally vulnerable is in that instant transformed into awe and relief. For we realize that God stood firm when we tried so frantically to push him away—not so he could destroy us or "control" us but in order to love us and help us find happiness. It is one of the most amazing surprises of the human pilgrimage.

As to what sort of response a person might make as he surrenders in the battle for the "God position" in his life, there are thousands of accounts. One classic statement is by Thomas à Kempis (1957, p. 253) from the thirteenth century: "O Lord, all thing that are in heaven and earth are thine. I desire to offer myself unto Thee, willingly and freely to be Thine forever . . . in the simplicity of my heart I offer myself unto Thee this day . . ."

A more contemporary statement might be this paraphrase of a nineteenth-century Christian's prayer of commitment: "Here, Lord, I abandon myself to you. I have tried in every way I could think of to manage myself, and to make myself what I thought I ought to be, but have always failed. Now I give it up to you. I give you permission to take entire possession of me." (See Smith 1952, p. 39.)

In many cases the response is not in words but is described as being dramatic but nonverbal: ". . . faith is here not so much believing this thing or that thing about God as it is hearing a voice that says, 'come unto me.' We hear the voice, and then we start to go without really knowing what to believe either about the voice or about ourselves; and yet we go. Faith is standing in the darkness and a hand is there, and we take it" (Buechner 1966, p. 42). Or imagine the pilgrim emotionally exhausted, isolated from himself and others through having tried to "recreate the world" to satisfy his own needs. From the darkness of his own mind he reaches out toward that which he thinks may be God. Sometimes at that moment people have spoken of a wave of light breaking into their darkness. It is as though a voice were saying through the light, "You are accepted. *You* are accepted, accepted by that which is greater than you . . ." [2]

As I have indicated, the language difficulties in trying to describe a profound conversion experience are enormous. I think Goethe may have been close to the mark when he said that the greatest truths can only be expressed dramatically. (God seems to have felt the same way in presenting the truth about himself in the Scriptures.) Perhaps only those who have been down this road to the point of surrender can easily recognize the landmarks and the language of response.

But whether the act of surrender is verbal or nonverbal, the subjective *experience* which follows is often a glorious one of *receiving* from God. It is like being released from an intense and frightening struggle for one's very life. For some people, that which is received is a great release from guilt, a sense of forgiveness and new relatedness. Others have gained a personal revelation of meaning to life. Some feel that they have been given the security, love, or esteem they have worked so hard for. Still others receive personal power, or perhaps a deep intuitive realization that at last they have the freedom to begin to become the self they vaguely dreamed possible—living in a less bound and more loving and creative way. But in almost every instance, that which is received seems in some inexplicable way to relate to the satisfying of the frantic needs one had tried so desperately to meet on his own. And the convert sees his world with different eyes.

---

2. See Paul Tillich (1949).

With a new perspective often comes a great wave of love for God and more particularly for Jesus Christ. There is a sense of loyalty and sometimes of being filled with the same spirit which was in Christ.[3]

As one "experiences" the gospel message in conversion, many of the basic questions about life are laid to rest. Is reality evil or gracious? Conversion indicates that it is gracious to the point of insane generosity. Is life meaningless or does it have a purpose? The new convert hears the reply of Jesus that not only does life have purpose but God has directly intervened in human events to convey the meaning of that purpose. What is the nature of the Really Real? Jesus' response is that the Really Real is generous, forgiving, saving love. In the end, will life triumph over death or death over life? The new follower of Jesus Christ is perfectly confident: The kingdom of his Father cannot be vanquished, not even by death.

Jesus is saying that in the end it will be all right, that nothing can hurt us permanently, that no suffering is irrevocable, that no loss is lasting, that no defeat is more than transitory, that no disappointment is conclusive.[4] And the new converted Christian tends to "know" these things are true, even though it may be years before he is able to articulate convincing reasons . . . if ever.

---

3. All converted Christians do not of course have the same sequence of events and feelings. For instance, some have a separate experience later in which they feel the overwhelming love of Jesus and the "filling" of their lives with his Holy Spirit.

4. See Andrew Greeley (1971, pp. 48, 49) for an elaboration of these ideas.

Seventeen

Becoming a Becomer

REGARDLESS of the circumstances surrounding a person's surrender, and whatever the specific "content" of his experience, there almost always follows a strange awareness that he has entered a whole new segment of his life—as if he had turned a page and begun a new chapter. Jesus said this fresh vision of life is like being "born again" (John 3:3). The recently converted Christian has a whole new cluster of motivating needs. He wants to become different from his past. And what this seems to mean in practical terms is that he is highly motivated to learn a whole new style of living. He feels that he is being liberated from many of the limitations of his past. His horizons have expanded, along with the possibilities of what he may become as a loving person. His old dominant values and the frantic sense of responsibility for his own success don't seem important as compared to learning about God and his will in ordinary life. And whether the convert's reaction of relief is expressed in booming laughter or silent tears, the inner feeling is one of *joy* and *gratitude*.

Different activities become very important. A new Christian finds himself learning to pray, reading the Scriptures, and relating in a more personal, vulnerable way to other Christians.[1] There is the pain of self-discovery through confession and honest interchange. But the characteristics of these new relationships with other becomers are those of the loving and affirming parents, brothers, and sisters one intuitively has felt could exist somewhere—for him. And with the availability of continuing *forgiveness*, the inner warfare loses much of its fearfulness and intensity.

It was this experience in my own life which made me realize that the nature (or at least the severe painfulness) of the superego's relation to the ego *can change*. As I truly accepted love and forgiveness from a heavenly Father, which I had not been able to accept from my human father, my response to God was that of a grateful adoring child.

My superego had originally been programed to conform to my human parents as seen through five-year-old eyes. But now a new process began. I wanted the values and perspective of *Christ* as a loving child wants those of his parents. And since God *could* get through to me with his forgiveness, my superego seemed to be getting *reprogramed*, at least to some extent. Old guilts subsided

---

1. These early tasks and disciplines are *very important*. At least they certainly have continued to be in my own life and the lives of most of those I know who have kept going. But having written *The Taste of New Wine* and two other books dealing more specifically with these early disciplines, I am not elaborating on them here.

through confession, forgiveness, and attempts at restitution. And as time went on, the "reminders" from my superego about my sins of commission and omission were not the terrible *condemnations* I'd always known. Rather it is as if a kind inner voice of a parent were saying, "Well, Keith, you blew it again. Want to confess and give life another try tomorrow?"

As the notion that we are forgiven and accepted "just as we are" sinks in, the false shame about our need for intimacy can subside. I'm *not* implying that becomers are amoral or that they are non-Christian in their sexual-ethical behavior. But they are more conscious of and grateful for the depth and richness of their human feelings. And they can experience their sexuality and personal relationships far more joyfully and freely within the Christian life. Besides the new freshness and depth of present relations, many have a sense of freedom and independence from neurotic *past* relationships and from exaggerated fears of other people's opinions.

And the inner verification of our acceptance by God can come to us through other Christians who know our past sin and failure and love us anyway. Their love may become the consummation of the inner longing for parental approval which has motivated so many of us through life.

All of these things make daily living much less anxiety-provoking. The neurotic need to repress our true feelings is not so great, and we are not under such tremendous pressure to find ultimate acceptance through our accomplishments.

Along with the dropping away of old interests and the picking up of new ones may come a new self-awareness. Since the converted person has confessed the worst sin— playing God—and been forgiven, he can now "afford" psychologically to begin seeing himself more nearly as he really is. He may become aware of faults he didn't dream he had *and of abilities and potentialities.* He may begin to see both faults and gifts he had repressed from consciousness because they were too threatening to his old self-image.

Ideally, a Christian minister should provide help for him in his pilgrimage of self-discovery and self-actualization as a child of God. This process can hardly be accomplished without the aid of a group of honest, loving, fellow becomers. And such a group can also help a person find the specific shape of his own creative ministry or function under God—whether it be vocationally religious or not.[2]

But here again a person is faced with a paradox. Although he may now be free to actualize that *unique* potential God has given him, his *hope* is that he will become more *like Christ* as he matures. And a strange thing seems to emerge—the more of his life he commits *to God,* the more *creative* and *unique* he may *appear* to be to others. People feel the Christ-like love of God coming through such a person, but *he* doesn't feel "like Jesus." He feels and looks *free* and interested in others.

---

2. The idea of a renewed church being made up of a strongly motivated group of "failures being made whole" is not new. Moses took a bunch of slaves for his key leaders (see Exod. 1:11f.); David began with a band of outcasts and outlaws who were to become the core of his army and the key leaders in his reign (1 Sam. 22:1, 2); Jesus built his kingdom on the lives of a dozen fearful men, the leader of whom denied him three times in his hour of greatest need (Matt 26:69–75). The common secret seems to involve the fact that only men whose sanity, security, and worth are founded on their continuing relation to God and each other are not "too busy" with their own kingdoms to be God's people in the world.

At a conference for ministers several years ago we were talking about Christian loving concern. One young man said, "I wonder how it would feel to love people *the way Jesus* did?" A silence followed. Then a white-haired minister said thoughtfully, "A Christian would probably never know. If you were loving people the way Jesus did, you'd be concentrating totally on the *other person and his problems* . . . and not on how you were feeling."

What this says to me is that an authentic Christian—becoming that person he was most nearly "designed" to be—does not *wind up* being an *imitator* when he becomes mature. Of course at first we must imitate other Christians as Paul suggested (Phil. 3:17). We have to pick up the openness and life-style of the Christian family way. But as a person becomes more committed to Christ and more transparent in being who he is, he does less posturing and imitating. This might mean, for instance, that the more totally and transparently I am being Keith Miller with you, *living for God,* the *more nearly* you will see *Jesus Christ through* me. And the Scriptures indicate that although we all receive the same Spirit and are to imitate God *in being loving, each* of us will be given the grace and the specific gifts we particularly need to grow up in Christ's perspective (see Eph. 4).

What all this means to me is that God is not making *imitations* of anything—even Jesus. He is creating authentic, original human beings who have the sound of Love in their lives and who unconsciously leave the fragrance of Christ behind them wherever they go. Over a hundred years ago Kierkegaard (1946, p. 49) tried to describe a whole Christian, but his contemporaries couldn't grasp the naturalness of the man he pictured. As the people commented on Kierkegaard's True Knight of the faith:

"Good God! Is this really he? Why he looks like an In-spector of Taxes! . . . he belongs wholly to the finite; and there is no townsman dressed in his Sunday best, who spends his Sunday afternoons in Fredericksburg, who treads the earth more firmly than he; he belongs altogether to the earth, no bourgeois more so. In him you will find no trace of that exquisite exclusiveness which distinguished the knight of the infinite. He takes pleasure in all things, takes part in everything, and everything he does, he does with the perseverance of earthly men whose souls hang fast to what they are doing."

The becomer may not feel all "Jesus like," but he does feel involved with life and with people in their misery and pain. And he wants to put their withered arms and hearts into God's hands.

Question IV

What About Christian Growth?

Eighteen

Christian Growth—
an Overgrown Trail

WHAT does it mean to "grow"? From the time I was a little boy, I was told, "You can do *that* when you get older . . ." And there were certain signposts of growth I can remember vividly, like the day I was allowed to ride my bicycle alone across the highway, or the first time I rode the bus downtown by myself. And much later, I remember the thrill of driving alone with a date after getting my driver's license at sixteen.

The same process of "growing" and waiting carries over into the adult world. The primary difference is that the criteria for growth have changed from increased age to ability and experience.

In almost all of the academic disciplines and in the professions today the notions of "growth" and "competence" have a central place. These terms seem to refer to the possession of an increasing amount of knowledge com-

bined with practice or experience until the professional
has reached a level considered by his colleagues to be
clearly superior. Visible status ladders have been devised
for him to climb: Grades are given, degrees granted,
societies are organized toward which the young professional can aim in order to demonstrate to his profession,
the world, and himself that he has personally attained
excellence in his field. People are called "Doctor," "President," "Senator," "Professor." Others demonstrate their
relative competence by the size of their net worth. But
since one cannot wear his balance sheet pinned to his
lapel, the wealthy have clothes, jewels, houses, cars, boats,
airplanes, trips, to indicate where they are on the financial
ladder. Professors use degrees, academic titles, research
papers, and books.

And this status system not only provides ways for the
people involved to measure advancement in their fields,
but it supplies the motivational power to help the young
professional pay the price it takes to get through the long
dry years of preparation to reach the higher rungs on the
ladder.

But what does *Christian* growth look like? Here we are
in a different world of relatedness. A Christian cannot
earn his status, his "righteousness," in his relationship to
God with any *amount* of effort or achievement. The gift
of God's love and acceptance is just that—a gift, an un-
earned gift, to be received or not.

According to the Scriptures, Christ loved us enough to
die for us before we even knew about him or wanted to
get our relationships straightened out (see Rom. 5:8). If
this is true, we certainly did not earn God's love through
conscious effort. But because our entire secular lives are

regulated by achievement goals and status systems, we in the church have done a strange thing: We have invented *invisible* status ladders for church members to climb to demonstrate their "growth" as compared to other Christians. The ladders are invisible because we know intuitively that we are not supposed to have them. But they are nevertheless very real—and I believe harmful—since they can keep us from genuine Christian growth and development.

Imagine with your mind's eye your own church's sanctuary with invisible ladders leaning against the walls. You can't see the ladders themselves, just people hanging there at various heights. Everyone who has been around a congregation long knows who the "head honchos," the acknowledged leaders, are. And yet there is often no formal designation of these people as the leading Christians —everyone in the community "just knows" they are on the higher rungs of the congregation's ladder.

But what do these ladders or criteria of growth "look like" in your church? If we do not know what the goals and unconsciously accepted directions for growth are, our Christian education efforts will be ineffective. They may be even self-defeating—especially if the programs aren't in line with people's preconceptions about what it takes to become a "better Christian."

I would like to describe a few of these "ladders" which are accepted, often without examination, as yardsticks for Christian growth and development.[1] In each case it is difficult to criticize the model since there is an important truth involved which *relates to* Christian

---

1. I am indebted to Dr. Findley Edge for some of the criteria and ideas in this discussion, learned from him in a private conversation in 1964.

maturity. The problem comes when the changed behavior advocated becomes a *status symbol* of growth.

The first "ladder" is built on the notion that Christian growth or goodness is determined by the "absence of badness" in a person's life. That is, one gets to be a better Christian according to the increasing number of *bad* things he does *not* do. For instance, if I don't drink, don't smoke, don't commit adultery, and don't dip snuff—and you don't drink, don't smoke, don't commit adultery but you *do* dip snuff, then I'm a better Christian than you are! But if carried to its logical conclusion, what would Christian perfection look like according to this model? Perfection would consist of lying in bed alone—inert—doing *nothing!* And of course that is a description of death, not life. Christian education programs bent in this direction tend to create a separatist, Pharisaical elite, as people get higher on the ladder.

It is dangerous to talk this way because I believe there *are* things we should *not* do, since they can damage our bodies and our relationships to God and people. But to make *not* doing these things *criteria for increasing righteousness* is to create a negative doctrine of "justification by works," since there is an implication that not doing bad things *earns* more righteousness.

Another "ladder" model indicates that Christian growth or goodness is determined by the number of *good* things one *does* as a Christian. And this is closer to many of us. According to this theory of growth, someone asks the pastor about a member of his congregation, "Is old Joe a good Christian?" The pastor may answer, "Oh, yes, he's in church *every* Sunday." The next rung on this activities ladder is attendance on Sunday nights, then on Wednesday nights (in churches which still have Wednesday night services). Perhaps the next rung might be teaching a Sunday school class or singing in the choir or leading the men's (or women's) organization of the church or being a vestryman. But when a lay person has done all these things—clear up to being head of the deacons or senior warden, he may go to his minister and say, "What's the next step, pastor? I want to be Christ's person." And the minister, thinking quickly back over his own ladder, says, "Why, George you must be *called to be a preacher!*"

Poor old George is horrified. He may have a speech impediment, hate counseling, or be a very inept leader. Yet, as Kenneth Chafin says, "We take up a collection, package him up, and mail him off to seminary." And often the truth is that the man has no business being an ordained minister. His witness and work as a *layman* might be much more fulfilling for him—and God. But because of the ladder, he goes to seminary. Then he discovers that there is a ministerial ladder to tell how he is doing as a pastor, compared to other pastors. It works something like this: You are at a gathering of ordained ministers after you've been out of seminary a few years, and an old classmate walks up. "Where are you serving now, George?" he says with a concerned look. (It is interesting to note that this question is almost always asked by a man in a large or prestigious church.) Old George stammers, "Arp, Texas."

"Oh, yes, *Arp*. How many people do you have there now (in your congregation)?"

"Seventy" (including three dogs in the yard and a couple of neighbor kids who play on the property during the service).

"Umm, well, I'm sure that's a great place to get *experience*." And he proceeds to tell poor old George about his

thriving and growing parish. This is called "rung dropping," and it tells the other person that he's lower than
you on the ladder.

After being a minister in an important church, the next
rung might be to become a district president or superintendent or even a bishop.[2] Fortunately the Lord seems to
have provided a way to by-pass the ministerial ladder:
One can go directly to the mission field from seminary,
and even the bishop doesn't know if he is holier than you.

Please do *not* misunderstand what I am saying. I think
we should attend worship and teach and work in the
church, and I thank God for people who are called into
the ordained ministry and to the mission field. But to
make *any* of these things criterion for earning growth-
status is to create an idol and a "works righteousness"
religion. I believe the gospel teaches that a young house-
wife serving coffee lovingly and happily to a neighbor in
Christ's name is *just as close to God* as a foreign missionary getting shot at in some far corner of the world. It may
be noble to go, but most missionaries *want* to go. And if
they are going to *earn status* with God or men through
their poverty or "giving alms in foreign lands," one
wonders how effective they could be anyway. I do not
believe that the works one does or the status one acquires,
as such, confer on him Christian maturity. (Although,
paradoxically, it is almost inevitable that a mature Christian *will* do good works.)

A third ladder of growth has to do with one's intellectual grasp of the faith. Although I believe that reading
and studying can help the process of Christian develop-

2. Each denomination has the rungs named differently, but
every one I've checked *has* the ladder—even the Quakers with
their "weighty friends" and those not so weighty.

ment immeasurably, intellectual pride is "a natural" for ladder climbers.

According to this theory, a person who knows more *about* his faith is thought to be more mature and closer to God. This ladder has a "conservative" and a "liberal" side. The conservative might feel that the more Bible verses he has memorized, the more mature he is. I have known some people who seemed to feel compelled to quote Scriptures when they met. Instead of saying "Good morning," they were more likely to say, "John 3:16." But in the building where my oil business friends have offices if you greeted them with "John 3:16," some men would think you were talking about the rest room on the third floor. These conspicuous Scripture quoters have a quotation for every remark.

Again, I hope you will not misunderstand what I am saying. I take the Scriptures *very* seriously, and I have many verses memorized. I find this helpful as an aid in living and as an index telling me where major themes of the faith are portrayed and discussed. And I use the Scriptures continually in teaching. But to make my ability and willingness to "memorize and quote" the criteria for growth and wholeness is, I believe, to misunderstand the gospel.

It has always been interesting to me to note that although Jesus used allusions to the Scriptures, he is reported to have *quoted* them primarily in his encounters with Satan (e.g., Matt. 4:1–11), when teaching and giving them a new interpretation (e.g., Matt. 5; 6; 7; 19:3–9, 26:31), or in direct confrontations when rebuking those who were unreal (e.g., Matt. 15:7–9). When talking to *the people,* he told stories about life to illustrate what God's purposes and reign would be like. Matthew (13:34) claimed that Jesus *only* used parables when speaking to the people. (See Matt. 13:3–9, 18–23, 24–30, 31–32, 33, 44, 45–46, 47–50; 18:23–35; 20:1–16; 21:33–45; 22:1–14; 25:1–13, 14–30, 31–46.)[3]

These things indicate to me that though the Scriptures were used for teaching purposes, they were *not* meant to be displayed as marks of righteousness. As a matter of fact, the Pharisees were criticized by Jesus for the pride they showed in carrying "Bible verses" prominently displayed in their phylacteries (Matt. 23:5).[4]

On the liberal side of the "knowledge" ladder Christians play "have you read?" Those who can discuss the latest book casting some light on the theological or psychological aspects of the faith are considered by this group to be the most mature Christians. At a meeting one man will insert into a conversation, "Last night I was reading Karl Olsson's book, *Come to the Party*. By the way, have you read it yet?" And the other Christian, defensive, not wanting to be considered "out of it," mumbles something like, "Well, I've heard of it. As a matter of fact, I think I *have* it, but I haven't had a chance to read it yet." And the other person says, "Oh, well, there's no reason you should have read it. No one

---

3. Since Matthew's bias was certainly *in the direction of* reference to Scripture, I checked only the first Gospel to give a general picture of the ways Jesus is reported to have communicated.

4. I have a few friends who quote the Bible continually and use this as an effective method of witnessing and evangelism. They are exceptional people and are so immersed in the Scriptures it seems natural for them. But for every one of these there are ten who come across to me as exhibitionists or users of an "in" language. I suppose I am making such a strong point about this because the Bible has meant so much to me, and I was almost driven away from it as a new Christian by a legalistic Bible quoter.

can read *everything*" (especially down there on the rung you're on. Of course, I'm a busy minister, too, but *I* managed to read it). And so it goes.

Harvard psychiatrist Paul Stern (1964, p. 48), talks about the ways a patient in therapy resists being known and thus healed. Of the defense mechanisms of the ego which keep people from depth encounter, one of the hardest for the therapist to get through is called "intellectualization." With this defense mechanism the patient knows so much *about* the technical jargon concerning his illness that his *articulateness* becomes his way to keep from coming to grips with the deeper *meanings* of his behavior. Thus he uses his knowledge as a shield against healing, love, and depth understanding of himself and others. And although I love to learn, I have often used knowledge *about* the Bible and theology as a way to avoid honest confession regarding my own weaknesses and personal questions.

This ladder of "knowledge about the faith" seems to be the principal criterion for Christian growth and maturity used in almost all theological seminaries, conservative and liberal.

There are many other status ladders which we Christians are climbing and using as criteria with which to determine our own growth and to judge and dismiss those who are "lower" or not even on our ladder.[5]

Some Christians have even made increasing poverty a ladder of virtue. There is little doubt in my mind that wealth is perhaps the most dangerous possession for a Christian to have if he wants to grow closer to God. But

---

5. At one time I made a ladder out of "honesty" and judged people's Christian maturity by how honest they were concerning their weaknesses and problems.

to make the *lack* of wealth a *mark* of Christian maturity is plainly an untenable notion. In the first place many Christian people are poor because of social oppression and lack of opportunities. Others are poor because of ignorance, bad business judgment, general incompetence, or even laziness—none of which are *signs* of increasing closeness to God or even *intention* in that direction.

A few years ago in some seminaries, as an example of another ladder, it was almost considered a cop-out to take an assignment as minister in a suburban church. The "social action" ladder was up, and a Christian's seriousness and maturity were judged by the proximity of his work to the ghetto. I believe there is no question about the fact that we in the church *must* be involved with the poor and the dispossessed. But to make even that involvement the measure of one's righteousness, one's closeness to God, is to create an idol. If a black (or white) minister, for instance, makes involvement in race relations the criterion for Christian commitment and growth, he may look down on (or dismiss as irrelevant) ministers who are called to some other part of the vocational vineyard— like pastoral counseling, teaching, or the parish ministry in areas where race is not the dominant problem. And such a judgmental attitude is psychologically no different from that of rung droppers on any other "works righteousness" ladder.

But if these ladders do not necessarily lead to maturity, then what does Christian growth look like? How does one become more free and available as the liberated person God made him to be in his healing ministry in the world?

Nineteen

Some Dead-end Paths

ALMOST everyone I know behaves as if he were on an uncharted and often unconscious search. We seem to be looking for what Paul Tournier (1968) calls a "place" that is ours particularly. When Jesus said, "In my father's house are many rooms"—and "I go to prepare a place for you" (see John 14), the implication is that in God's economy there is an emotional niche for me. But as I indicated earlier, we tend to believe that "place" will be a particular status on some achievement ladder—a particular job or income, a certain mate, through which or with whom I will experience a sense of complete acceptance and love. And so we climb the ladders we choose, or those our parents have chosen for us.

But so often on this search, when I have gotten where I thought my place of peace and fulfillment would be, it has moved on ahead of me, like a mirage across the desert. When I first started to work after college, I thought that when the time came at which I was earning $500.00 a month, I'd feel secure financially. But when that day arrived, the figure had moved ahead of me and I needed $750.00, and so on.

A man once told me that he and his wife had been going through "hell." He was a person with a great deal of ability, was president of his own company at a very early age, had married a lovely girl, and they had a houseful of cute children about as fast as they could. Then they became Christians. But even as Christians they continued to argue and fight almost constantly. Finally they had a confrontation in which he said something to the effect that: "We're fighting all the time. What's the matter with *you?*" She was defensive and blurted out, "It's this *house.* It's so small, and we don't have any privacy." The husband was in a rapid financial climb, and during the next few years he built his wife four new houses—each larger than the one before. "Finally," he said, remembering, "I built her a beautiful fifteen-room home in the nicest area of our city. And after the mover left, we sat down in the living room of that lovely home—and had the *worst fight of our marriage.* Right then," he continued, "I realized our problem *wasn't* the house."

But the tragedy is that many of us never get in a position to discover that, so we keep striving for material things, hoping against hope that they will give us security or esteem. But when people realize that the reaching of a material goal or status is not the "solution" or consummation of life—not necessarily the finding of a spiritual or emotional "place"—a real identity crisis can arise. And this type of crisis has reached almost epidemic proportions in America because so many people are achieving their material goals at an early age.

As I indicated in chapter fifteen, this type of crisis can

lead a pagan to a confrontation with God. But the same crisis can also happen to *Christians* who are not likely to see the crisis in terms of a need for conversion or surrender.

All my life I have been counting on the reaching of a nebulous goal to bring me the inner sense of assurance that I am "O.K." And even as a Christian I've sought the ultimate self-acceptance and security I have always longed for and felt must exist. I tried climbing some of the "ladders" I found in the church. And the striving activity toward the goals had at least one good effect: It kept me from succumbing to loneliness and anxiety behind the facade.

But when I set a life goal and *reach* it, and it does not bring final security and self-acceptance, then I am left with a strange inner destitution. I have exploded my latest hope which has motivated me to go on through the frightening emotional thicket of compulsive modern life.

Mothers have told me that for twenty to thirty years they worked and prayed for the day when their children would be safely raised and on their own. All their energies and planning were directed toward this goal. They found themselves saying to their husbands, "Won't it be *great* when the children are grown?" But when the day actually came, a great depression followed. The "meaning of life" went out the door with the last child. I have heard similar stories from a new district superintendent in the church who had always dreamed of being one, from a corporation president who had given twenty years of his life to "arrive," and from a world-famous athlete who reached the pinnacle of his field. All experienced great depressions when they reached their goals—and all were outstanding Christian leaders.

Some of us have a tricky device we use to avoid despair

in the event we don't find happiness on the road we've chosen. In our fantasy life we save an emotional "goodie" to dream about for a rainy day. We say to ourselves, "Some day I'm going to learn to paint or be a sculptor, run away with another woman, or write a book." Then in our minds, in case we fail to gain fulfillment on the road we've taken, we can live in our fantasy and tell ourselves there is another road we could have taken successfully—and which we may still take in the event of the failure of our present tactics. In my case as a businessman, I kept in reserve the idea that some day I would write a book, and that would bring fulfillment. But through a series of unforeseen circumstances, my bluff was called and I actually wrote a book. Then people began to read the book. It got more attention than I had dreamed it might, and I had a real depression.

I was baffled . . . until I realized that I had used up my escape hatch to "total consummation." Now I had to deal with my present reality situation for any hope of genuine fulfillment. Because as meaningful as writing is to me, I saw that there is *no* status, no spiritual or emotional closure point in life at which one attains "total fulfill-ment." I saw that the purpose of growth was not a "state" or "end" at all. And I began to realize that something very important must be missing in my sense of direction and my goals as a Christian.

In the conversion crisis of my life I had seen my total self-centeredness. And after great struggle and fear, I finally confessed and surrendered to God. Although I still recognized that the world was a frightening jungle in which the future is uncertain, I also felt that ultimately I was "safe" because I was somehow personally accepted by God. I realized that my life is only stable in a rootless world because it is now attached to God, the one stable center, through Jesus Christ. And I was not alone. Through Christ I was connected with struggling brothers and sisters who had also found purpose in trying to become God's people and to participate in his will in the world.

For a few years I felt marvelous. I have always been a careful manipulator, and I began to feel free to take a few risks in order to relate to people. In the process a number of changes were taking place in my attitudes and behavior. And in order to try to "grow" as a Christian I climbed every spiritual ladder in sight. I began to speak at lay meetings, large and small, and was filled with a sense of newness and "joy."

But then something happened. I got sick of Christians. Everywhere I went people were so "good" and so "victorious." They talked about their "victories" and said, "Give God the glory," but the way they came across to me was, "Look how good I am—with God's help, of course." There seemed to be an implication that they had "arrived" and were now "full grown" in Christ. And I was somehow ashamed to be one of them, since we seemed to have an arrogance about our commitment, as if we should have special recognition or credit for surrendering to God. I got bored with Christian meetings and tired of the sound of my own voice—and my family joined me. At conferences I seemed to be repeating old responses automatically rather than listening and responding within the moment. I knew that some of this was inevitable for a traveling speaker, but communicating what I believed became a matter of "going to meetings" continually. And these highly stimulating meetings were like a steady diet of cake icing which soon turned to acid in the stomach when I got back to the job of vocational coping. I began to long for the solid oatmeal of daily gut-level living.

But what does one do? How do you grow after making the most total surrender you know how and trying to climb every "ladder" in sight? I began to ask people. Occasionally someone would respond with, "I'll pray for you," which was kind of them. I wish someone had said, "I've got the same problem. Let's pray together for help." Because, as it was, their prayers became a kind of rung dropping which left me feeling even more lonely and inadequate.

Then I found some people who were able to tell me the next step. They said I had committed my life to Christ as *Savior*, but the next move was to commit it to him as *Lord*. Other people spoke of the same process as my needing the "second blessing" or to be "filled with the Holy Spirit." But in each case it amounted to the need for a *"total commitment,"* a *"total* surrender" of one's self and will to God. He then would fill me with his Spirit and the special gifts necessary to live as a part of Christ's Body on earth. This seemed to make sense and still does. And after some thought, I made the second commitment—to Christ as Lord. This experience is often called being filled with the Holy Spirit and is sometimes accompanied by charismatic gifts pertaining to such things as evangelism, being a pastor or teacher, healing, or speaking in tongues. But before long I learned a jarring lesson: I was on what amounted to a "Holy Spirit ladder." If I have received a certain "spiritual gift" which you have not, and talk about it in my public "witness," there is a subtle implication that I must be more mature or closer to God than you—even if you have made a total commitment to Jesus Christ. Or if

you have received gifts I have not, I find myself concentrating on getting those gifts for me—instead of loving
people and working for justice in the world.

Along with the filling of the Holy Spirit commitment
came a way to banish problems of pride and self-centeredness which had continued to plague me in some of my
most important relationships after my conversion. This
method or technique of getting rid of pride and self-
centeredness has several descriptions. And it includes a
valuable truth. But when such a technique is presented
as an infallible way to keep pure, it can easily lead to
phoniness and rung-dropping guilt.

One description goes something like this: Man's mind
or life is described as a circle with a chair or throne in the
center. Man begins life sitting on the throne, that is, he
is in charge of his life, being the "king." When he first
"asks Christ to come into his life as Savior," then God
gets into the circle, but the person himself is still on the
throne. The second commitment, or being filled with the
Holy Spirit, happens when the person, through an act of
the will, "gets off the throne and puts Christ on it." After
that, when the "Spirit-filled" person has a resentment,
lust, hate, etc., he realizes that he has replaced Christ as
Lord of his life and by an act of his will simply puts
Christ back on the throne and submits to him. This
simple illustration provided a sacramental way to handle
many problems. And for months I virtually didn't have
any problems.

But one morning I woke up with a huge resentment. I
realized I was on the throne, got off, put Christ on the
throne, and sat there on the floor in the throne room with
the *same big resentment*. I realized that I had been taught
that if I were full of the Holy Spirit I would always be

able to submit to him at will, that is, to *control my feelings,* through this device I have described. And when I could not, I was forced to *repress* my true feelings from my consciousness, since to admit to not being able to give them to Christ would be to admit I was not *really* full of the Holy Spirit.

So, in a moment of honest agony I realized that no man can manipulate God into giving him different *feelings.* All legitimate spiritual gifts—including exalted feelings—are the result of God's grace. All I can do is submit my *real* feelings of resentment and tell him it is my desire that these *not* be so. But then I must go about my business and try to change my *behavior,* waiting on God's timing as to *when* and *if* my feelings will change. As a student of psychology and as a Christian, I knew that one cannot *force* his *feelings* to change—even for God's sake. The psychologist Jolande Jacobe (1962, p. 124), speaking for Carl Jung, said that "the widely prevailing view that psychic development leads ultimately to a state in which there is no suffering is of course utterly false. Suffering and conflict are a part of life; they must not be regarded as 'ailments'; they are the natural attributes of all human existence, the normal counterpole, so to speak, of happiness. Only when from weakness, cowardice, or lack of understanding the individual tries to evade them do ailments and complexes arise."[1]

After trying both consciously and unconsciously to earn, or manipulate God's increasing approval in my direction in all the ways I've described, I began to realize that I had deeply misunderstood the process of Christian growth.

---

1. For an excellent biblical basis for a similar conclusion about the Christian life, see John Knox's (1966) book on Romans, Chapters 5-8: *Life in Christ Jesus.*

Twenty

Growth:
a New Look
at "A Leap of Faith"

IN order to see if I could determine what Christian growth might look like in the Scriptures, I went back and studied the lives of the greatest heroes of the faith in the Bible. As I began to look across the whole careers of men like Abraham, Moses, and even Jesus, I realized that spiritual development in the biblical tradition was very different from the things I'd tried. It was at about that time that I read a book by Dr. Paul Tournier (1968) called *A Place for You*. As I was reading, I realized that Christian "progress" on the adventure with God is not reaching a pinnacle, nor ladder-climbing, nor straining neurotically for doctrinal or moral purity, nor ecstatic experiences.

I began to grasp the notion that Christian growth may take place through continuing to surrender our ultimate securities as they are revealed to us. We begin at conversion by renouncing the flimsy but familiar security of our pagan existence: the role of God in our own vocational or social worlds. As we turn our backs on the past, we realize that we have tried to build a life on the shifting sand of our achievements. By turning loose of our compulsive "kingdom building" our hands are free. And we can begin to live a new life on Christ's promise of ultimate security and love.

But almost immediately, it seems, we begin to build, instead, a new controllable security by climbing one of the Christian status ladders. And when we see that we have started building a competitive kingdom again, we must surrender and repent.

If this is true, then Christian growth may take place through an "endless" series of turning loose of our more controllable securities *as ultimate*. In the act of turning loose we reach out with a leap of faith which is always frightening, always to some degree anxiety-provoking. And with newly freed hands we can reach out creatively to touch God's people in healing ways.

Pierre Teilhard de Chardin has indicated that this kind of relinquishment is a perfect preparation for death. For at the end of life the Christian who has surrendered all material and status securities as ultimate has only to turn loose of the body to be unencumbered in joining God.

But is this scriptural—this idea that growth takes place through surrendering abilities, status, techniques, and awards? Are we supposed to release these things which are less than God but which we have clutched to save ourselves and build ourselves up? Paul Tournier (1968) suggests that this view is biblical. Look at Abraham. He was a man who evidently had a secure place with his father in Ur and then in Haran. But the Scriptures indicate that God asked him to turn loose of that place and go to a foreign land in which his safety and future would be uncertain. He did, and God gave him the security of a new place in what was to become Palestine.

Then Abraham wanted the assurance of the continuation of his "name" through a son. And in his old age he and Sarah had a son. In at least one way this son meant more to Abraham than a son might to a Christian today. At that time the idea of heaven was not a part of the Hebrews' thinking. Heaven was, as I understand it, a rather late idea in biblical history. When an ancient Hebrew died, the only "afterlife" he had to look forward to might be the vague land of shadows (*Sheol*). His only hope to live beyond his own death was through a son. So in the story when Abraham was asked to sacrifice his son, Isaac, on the altar, it was something like asking him to give up his only child *and heaven*. And his willingness to turn loose of this kind of security in order to trust God made him the model of the man of faith for all future generations (see Rom. 4:1–25).

A similar pattern unfolds in the life of Moses. He was raised in a position of affluence and power, but was confronted by God with risking his position to help his own people. Then he ran away and found a new security and a family with the Kenites. But he was asked to turn loose of that safe place, confront the Egyptian pharaoh, and lead the people out of Egypt. After much struggling with God and himself, he turned loose and went. And finally, at the end of his adventures in the wilderness, just as he was arriving at the promised destination, he was asked to surrender his place with the people and not to go into Palestine with them. Moses did let go, and he became the greatest spiritual hero of the Jewish people. He and Abraham seemed to grow in spiritual stature each time they released their security and took a new leap of faith in trying to do God's will with their lives.

In Jesus' life there is a similar struggle and outcome. At Gethsemane Jesus evidently felt that his ministry was at stake. A week earlier the people had welcomed him into Jerusalem with palm branches, hailing him as the Messiah. He was apparently fulfilling his dream, and was being accepted by the people. And yet at Gethsemane Jesus evidently heard God saying, "Turn loose of your ministry and mission and trust their safety and yours to me alone." Three times the Scriptures indicate that Jesus tried to talk God out of that course. But the call was to "turn loose." He did, and the Christian Church is here bearing his name at least partially because he did surrender that night.

A Christian, according to this view of Tournier's, is like a person hanging from a trapeze bar. And that bar is whatever your security is truly invested in—though a Christian often consciously *believes* that his security is in Christ. But in my case, my *true* trust has most often been in things like social acceptance and my ability to earn a decent living. Most of my deepest concentration and time have been occupied in enhancing and protecting those things which constitute my real, though often unconscious, securities at any given time. And growth takes place when God swings another trapeze bar in view. The new trapeze might be a vocational challenge, a chance to be more honest in my work or to risk financial security in order to do his will. The "bar" coming toward me might be a sense of calling to lead a more disciplined life with Christ, or help some oppressed people—and risk rejection.

But there are two basic problems we face as we are confronted by a call to relinquish our present equilibrium and reach out: One difficulty is that the new challenge (which will be the scene of our security *later*) usually appears *at first* as a frightening *threat*. To grasp any new situation which will include our security base one must let go of the old, it seems. The new trapeze bar swings toward me just far enough from the present one that I cannot hang on with one hand and grab the new while still clinging to the old. So each new opportunity to grow carries with it a decision to surrender an old security as ultimate. But each new decision also represents a chance to place one's trust more deeply in God's hands through a very threatening leap of faith. And the risk is always frightening, if a real security is at stake. There is inevitably a kind of death involved in each significant spurt of growth.[1]

People have paid thousands of dollars over the centuries to watch trapeze artists, not because it is difficult to hang from a bar. They pay for that one second when the performer lets go and reaches for the next bar. Will he fall? And I believe that's *our* question in the church! I think many of us want to surrender our flimsy securities

1. Just a word of caution for Christian leaders who may take this position seriously. Some people are far more *prone* to risk than others. Each person has a particular pace and rhythm at which he grows and learns best. For a Christian leader to try to *force* risking on the part of others is neither effective nor safe in my opinion. The leader can risk in his own life and can tell stories of others' risking. But he should realize that not only is each individual evidently different from others with regard to the size, frequency, or even possibility of his risking, but that there is also a rhythm of growth and withdrawal *within* any given life. Pierre Teilhard de Chardin (1968, p. 94) said, "There is a time for growth and a time for diminishment in the lives of each one of us. At one moment the dominant note is one of constructive human effort, and at another mystical annihilation. . . ." (See also Eccles. 3:1–9.)

and reach ahead for a deeper and more personal involvement with God and his people—with life. But we are
afraid that if we turn loose, we will fall into an unknown
condition and lose what we have—and we cannot chance
it.

One of the most fascinating and bewildering discoveries
Freud made about our minds is that we will often resist
being healed of painful neurotic limitations. People cling
to miserable anxieties and crippling physical symptoms
rather than risk the responsibility of living with a new
freedom which might enhance their lives and unbind their
creativity. *We would often rather have a miserable condition with which we are familiar than a glorious but uncertain one.*

But if this *is* the course of Christian growth for becomers—this turning loose and reaching out—what
provides the motivation to move ahead? How does a
Christian speaker or counselor help people to release and
leap? I can personally vouch for the fact that telling
people they "ought to" has very little effect (at least it
never has on me). Why can't we learn to risk it as we are
challenged to do from the pulpit year after year? What
makes us become willing to turn loose of present securities for Christ's sake?

Several years ago I was talking with some psychologists
concerning information on human motivation which came
out of the Second World War. They said that certain
studies were made of men's behavior under combat conditions and later checked against similar experiences in non-
threatening circumstances.

For instance, imagine with me that we are on a Euro-
pean tour together with about forty other people in a
tour bus. We have stopped on a hillside outside a small

ancient city in southern Italy. The tour leader is explaining our plan to "sight-see" in the city. He tells us of the old walls along the narrow streets, of the gnarled trees which often grow together over the cobblestones. He talks about the stone cathedral with the long slit windows where the early defenders could pour boiling oil on anyone trying to force entry. And the guide tells us that if we get separated we will meet at 5:00 P.M. at a small square named "Navonne." After such a briefing, questionnaires were passed out to find out how much people remembered about the communication they received from their tour leader. Amazingly little, it seems. They knew they were going into town anyway and simply didn't listen to the details.

Now let me change the situation slightly. We are the same group—only *this time* it is in the midst of the Second World War and we are part of an American fighting force moving through Italy. Our commanding officer has told us that we are going to move into the same small Italian city—only there are enemy snipers still holed up there, and we're to try to drive them out or kill them. *Now* he describes the walls along the streets (behind which a sniper could crouch) and the trees which grow together (in which a soldier could hide) and the cathedral with the slit windows (which could house a machine gunner). "And if anyone gets separated from his outfit, we are leaving from a small square called 'Navonne' at 1700 hours." Before the unit moved out they were tested as to how much of the description of the city they remembered —*almost total recall!*

It seems that we learn and remember things when our *own personal destinies* are wrapped up in our learning and remembering them. And my experience has been that I am generally willing to be vulnerable and risk myself for other people only when my new experience of life and destiny with God seems to call for this kind of vulnerability.

This turning loose and risking has some amazing *educational* side effects: When I step forward and become vulnerable to people out of gratitude to God for saving my sanity and loving me, *then* I am forced back to a deeper interior prayer life and to reading the Scriptures. Because when I really risk, I am over my head, out of my depth, and I *need* more power and insight in order to *survive* each day. When I study or hear sermons at such times, I am highly motivated and much more likely to retain what I am reading or hearing.

As Kenneth Chafin has said, "We pray for power in the church all the time, but we don't need more power to do most of the safe things we do in the church—just more money and volunteers." But when we *must* have power and discernment, we pray for it and work for it. And *that's* when it seems to come.

In our small group of becomers I was forced to this amazingly simple discovery about "Christian education." For years I had been *urging* men and women to study the Bible, pray, and attend church so they could become "stronger in the faith." And all they did was resist my efforts. But as members of our group actually began to risk themselves and their securities, they started *asking* how they could learn more about the Scriptures, theology, and prayer. And I realized that for many lay people motivation to get "educated about the faith" is a natural *by*-product of a vulnerable life-style. If a Christian is *consciously* in need of God, because he is risking his safety, he is highly motivated to learn what the tools and content of his faith are.

I am aware that you may be saying it would be possible for a group of Christians to create a growth "ladder" out of "turning loose," on which the members would indulge in "competitive surrendering." And of course this is a possibility. But as a student of psychology and the church, I do not look for any mass movement in which an individual actually releases that security on which he has depended for his emotional safety. The sort of surrendering of which I am speaking here is often as agonizing as that taking place at conversion.

Twenty-One

Turning Loose—

to Free the Hands

for Loving ... and Becoming

WHAT does turning loose feel like for the one growing?

If it is true that Christian growth involves risking, then
what inner process does one go through to release a security which has become more important than doing God's
will?[1]

In looking back over my own life, I realize that sometimes a challenge has been presented to me in a specific
and unavoidable way. For instance, an invitation to teach
communication and counseling at a particular graduate

---

1. The participants in the human potential movement in psychology have shown us that significant behavioral change by an
individual involves not only intellectual understanding but often
also emotional commitment, vulnerability, and the process of
personal risking (e.g., see Carl Rogers [1970] *On Encounter
Groups,* and William Schutz [1971] *Here Comes Everybody*).

school arrived. After careful consideration it seemed right that I should go. Suddenly I had to *decide* whether or not to risk leaving the city I lived in with the security of place for me and our family, whether to risk cutting my income by moving, etc. In other words, I had to decide whether the proposed opportunity was right *enough* for me to rip up my family by the roots *for the seventeenth time.* An emotional involvement and decision to risk had been precipitated from "the outside" by way of the invitation to teach.

But what if one is restless with his life and ministry, would like to analyze his present priorities and security base, but *no confrontation comes from the outside?* How would he go about it? Strangely, I have found something akin to the crisis leading to conversion in each new episode involving the possibility of growth. As this statement implies, I believe significant Christian growth is sporadic and comes as a result of major or minor confrontations and decisions.[2]

After initially surrendering to God in my desperation, I was exhausted from the struggle. Gradually I began to regain some enthusiasm, health, and strength. But during the next few years, I started (unconsciously) building a new kingdom for myself—this time a "Christian kingdom" as a lay witness. When I recognized what had happened,

---

2. Even a decision to "take a class" involves a commitment of time and the risk of failure. One must release his security as a "non-failer" in that subject to enter the class. *The growth takes place through the work following as well as in the decision.* But the decision process and initial "leap" set it off. According to Seward Hiltner (1949), the first thing we know about religious development is that, whatever its specific nature, it is not a mere unfolding . . . "it has spurts, plateaus, dips. It contains optimal occasions. . . ."

I got sick of myself and had to struggle again through the crisis of surrender in order to grow in Christ. That's why the notion of a second commitment (or being filled with the Holy Spirit) seemed so right.

But I am finding that over the years I must die to *many* succeeding idols and securities as they become the fortresses behind which I protect myself as god in my life (see Luke 9:23, 24). The maintenance of these securities makes me overly cautious. And protecting myself keeps me from the vulnerability of walking unarmed into people's hearts and lives. But I resist the process of risking. And at each point of growth or release I want to stop and build a permanent "home" to live in. I keep forgetting to "consider the lilies of the field. . . ."

And because I often repress from my own consciousness any traits or even behaviors which don't fit my picture of what I think I *ought* to be, I have a very difficult time coming to a growth crisis by myself. As a lay teacher or "Christian writer," it is especially difficult for me to admit that I am playing God in the *new world* of friends, opportunities, and "ministries" available to me now— which were not even live *possibilities* at the time of initial "surrender." So I resist discovering my own new *Christian* idols . . . and thus avoid the danger of risking them. Of course by doing this I may also be avoiding the possibility of gaining a clearer sensitivity to the best direction for my life and ministry.

As a first step in a self-examination to try to discover what my own "protected security" might be, I have asked myself: "What, *next to God,* is my most important asset or relationship which I'd hate most to face the future *without?*"[3] I've even found it helpful to list the most important things in my life on a piece of paper. But here

---

3. Because of my own history of repression and denial with

again, in my case, repression often takes over, and the list may look different than my *actual* daily priorities would indicate. So I have learned to check in the area of my private and unedited thoughts and behavior to determine the *true* source of my priorities and securities.

One way I have found helpful was proposed some years ago by a friend named Fred Smith. He suggested that we ask ourselves things like: "What specific kinds of articles do I read in the newspaper every day?" And as I thought about this idea the first time, I realized that I read the same sections in almost every paper I pick up.

Do you find yourself concentrating almost exclusively on the sports page, the war headlines, stories about murder and rape, the financial page, the society section, the religious news, the editorials, or the funnies when you only have a limited time? In my case it seems that the things my mind continually selects to read when it is *free to choose* (and no one is watching) indicate or provide clues to my true interests, values, needs, and securities.

Another way I have found to locate the real focus of my life is to ask, "What do I *think about* again and again when I am alone or my mind is not occupied with work or conversation?" For example, at different times I have found myself absorbed with recurring thoughts about such things as my work, my "ministry" (or "witness"), my wife, sexual fantasies, our children, and acceptance by certain people. At other periods my thoughts, when I am alone, have centered in my own specific personal problems —jealousy, resentment, fear of failure, death, etc.

Over any extended period of time the thing my mind

---

regard to admitting that I am playing God, I've found it helpful to give God first place in asking the question, realizing that whatever *I* list as *second* is very likely even *more* important than God to me *as a priority motivating my actual behavior.*

grasps, clings to, thinks about with intensity (when it is free to think of anything at all), is very likely that thing which is most important, or *God*, to me.[4] This is a rather horrifying concept. People have said to me, "Do you mean to say that it is wrong to love my *Christian ministry* more than anything?" And mothers, especially, have asked, "Are you saying that it is not right to love my child more than anything in the world?" My answer in both cases is: "Yes, I believe it is wrong." Because whatever we really value most is for all practical purposes our *god*, and as such it becomes our security and the ultimate checkmate for all our decisions. I have been a member of a church in which the minister loved his ministry more than anything else. And he did a good job *as long as* everything went exactly according to his plan. But when people disagreed or decided to go another way with the church's program, he got frantic. He had to manipulate dishonestly and do things he had never done "for God's sake" to protect his vision of his ministry. We sensed somehow that he was doing it all for himself, and we didn't want to help him . . . even though at the time we didn't know why, since he had a reputation as a dedicated and godly man.

A man who makes a god out of his ministry (or anything except God) may eventually ruin the object of his worship. A woman who loves her child (or husband) most, unconsciously puts on the shoulders of that child

---

4. Since we tend to repress our unacceptable goals and values, the recurring thought or subject matter in the newspaper *may* be only a symptom of the deeper more dominant goal or security. And since our minds are not *consciously* guided to certain thoughts or articles, we can often "slip past" our psychological defenses by these methods of self-examination and locate our unconscious controlling motivations.

(or husband) the *responsibility for her happiness.* And many children rebel frantically from such demands, telling their mother in loud, clear behavior that they are not and cannot fulfill her life or her expectations. And the child is *right*—no human being can fulfill the role of God for another. I am convinced that in America we have thousands, if not hundreds of thousands, of forty-year-old children who are ruining their own marriages because they never would make the break from a mother "who just worshiped me."

But what if a Christian discovers that he has made a security idol out of something good which is less than God? In the first place, his attachment to that person or thing he worships will become the "price" of his integrity. A minister who worships his parish ministry will get involved in social issues such as race relations, for instance, only until his involvement threatens the security of those parishioners who might negatively affect his ministry. A worshiping mother will let her son have all the freedom he wants to grow *until* his choices threaten her vision of what the child should be.

What can be done when a person sees that the basic focus of his interest and security is centered on something less than God? The next step for me seems to be *confession.* I have to admit to myself and to God that I want my own will for me and the people around me. And I must face the fact that I am clinging to and protecting an idol—my ability, my work, a relationship, a goal—as my real security in which I'm putting my faith and energy. In other words, I have to tell God that I really love and trust something more than him.

My own most recent idol has been writing. I have found that I have a fantasy of wanting to be a famous writer.

At first I laughed at this as a normal kind of thought for an egomaniac who has had a book published. But as the thought recurred, I quit laughing. I found that I was getting angry with anyone who interrupted my writing, whereas I had always been open to people coming to me for help or to visit. I got impatient with my family. And I began resenting those parts of my work not connected directly with writing. But I continued doing all the traveling, speaking, etc., I'd been doing. Finally I got miserable enough to stop and see what had happened: I had very subtly and unconsciously made "becoming an outstanding writer" the highest value in my life. Since this was my god, all other values and relationships had to be brought in line with it. My family, friends, students, and strangers had either to support my god or be somehow pushed into the background. And they were. But it all turned sour in my mouth and made me frustrated and very lonely in a way I didn't understand. Fortunately they were all still "present" and trying to relate to me.

Finally I came to the point at which I realized that writing had become my bet for ultimate security—instead of God and his grace. My knuckles were white from clinging to that "trapeze bar"—the dream of being a great writer. I had a terrible time admitting this to myself. I said, "This is ridiculous. Of course I love God more. I'm just a dedicated writer, that's all." But my behavior gave me away. So I finally confessed: "God, I would like to be an outstanding writer more than I want to be your person." This sounds so childish and naïve as I write it. And I almost did not tell you. But I think the subtlety and unacceptable nature of our idolatry is part of the reason we haven't been able to face it in the church.

The third thing I think one does is to *surrender again—*

totally: "God, I want you more than I want to be an out-standing writer. I want to know you and do your will, trusting you with the outcome of my efforts and my life." But the first time I started to say those words about writing, I realized I could not say them honestly. As stupid as it sounds, there was a stubborn knot in my insides which said, "No, I'm *not* giving this up to you, God. I want it for *me*—even if it ruins my life."

But I knew myself well enough to know it would ruin my life if I kept it in the number one position. So I finally said, "God, I *can't* turn loose of my dream. But I *want* to. I give it up to you *by intention* and give you permission to come into the deeper layers of my personality and help me turn loose and reach toward you for my ultimate security and meaning. I want to write if it's your will, but I want to become your person more." I realized in that moment that I had committed everything *over which I had control* to God.

Slowly my life began to take on a new shape. I actually have become a more disciplined writer and am spending more hours writing. This has meant planning my time more carefully and some painful "no" saying to other kinds of activities. I have the feeling that my job is only to become whatever God wants me to be . . . which right now seems to include writing. But whether anyone reads what I write or thinks I'm great for having written it is God's problem . . . most of the time.

I am finding that my "place" in which I can hope to risk and grow is *not* a committed status at which I arrived through conversion. Nor is it the top of a ladder of works I've performed. My "place," paradoxically, is not a "des-tination" at all. But it feels like a moving journey, a changing pilgrimage with a group of broken but joyous becomers. We are weak and yet know the power that comes from being personal. We have been broken in that our kingdoms have been surrendered. And yet we are in the process of becoming whole as we reach out with open and creative hands toward people, work, and God.

I see Jesus Christ as our Lord, our model. He is the tour guide on this lengthening adventure to show us God's kingdom and to introduce us to *all* his people. And what we give to others "along the road" is that which we have received: forgiveness, hope, esteem, security, love, possessions, and the possibility of creative self-actualization, as we commit our lives to Christ and to each other.

But to go with him, I must be willing to move out into the world and turn loose of one status, one prejudice, one possession at a time when it becomes more important than Jesus Christ and his journey. For I believe that Christ continues to live vulnerably as he moves across history at the growing edge of the present moment—whether we in the church do or not.

Epilogue

Into the World—
Prophets or Lovers?

What is all this "becoming" for? I mean, what is the purpose and direction of the self-actualizing Christian in the world?

Recently I attended a meeting in Houston, Texas, called *Meaning and Belonging: New Patterns for the Church.* The purpose of the five-day-gathering was to try to uncover some directions the church might take in the future. People from very different backgrounds came to discuss their views and listen for feasible new sounds.

From the first evening there was a kind of electricity in the air. There were twenty-one speakers, and without hostility or evidence of "superiority," one after another addressed the 900 participants. They did it with conviction, humor, and piercing insight. I was confronted to my toes by the prophetic voices and deeply moved by those finding community and loving concern in local situations.

After three days I saw a Christian archetype evolving from the presentations—not an outline of a proposed *program* for the future (which I had expected) but a sketch of a proposed *person*. In my mind for the first time was a dreamlike composite of the man or woman who just might be able to move into the future and free other people in our kind of society.

For a while it looked as if the Christian of the future was going to turn out to be an utterly fearless social prophet. One of the most incisive prophetic sparks was struck by William Stringfellow. As he spoke, it became clear to me that some Christian leaders of tomorrow must have guts and insight concerning the forces and power structures involved in the *political* activities as well as the personal and social agony of their country. Stringfellow spoke of the essential need for charismatic gifts from God for those who attempt to work in the political and social structures. And the primary gift he cited was *discernment:* the gift of being able to recognize *evil* in the guise of *goodness,* and *hope* and *meaning* in *apparent failure.* For without the gift of discernment it was apparent that all the other charismatic gifts can quickly become misused and divisive.

I became discouraged at that point because I am not a political or social prophet, and because I have always distrusted people who *decide ahead of time* to be prophets. They seem to have a god-shaped chip on their shoulders. But the prophetic people on this program did not. So I was frustrated and felt the inner confusion and pain of changing my mind. Yet I knew that there was something missing about the clear call to be prophets.

And this talk about being prophetic was frightening. I realized that not everyone would be called to confront the political structures, but it was clear that *some* would. And I had the uneasy feeling that I should at least be willing to consider doing what I could. On the other hand, I knew that the personal vulnerable life-style of the becomers was the only hope I had of finding the courage and freedom to even try to risk speaking out. I could not see giving up the personal healing strength for the acid power of the prophetic life-style. A choice seemed to be looming.

As the personal, small group advocates spoke, I realized what was missing. These speakers alluded to the almost universal loneliness and restlessness, the need for love, personal affirmation, and meaning. And the point was made that people are motivated almost exclusively by those who touch their personal needs. I saw that any prophet who hopes to be effective in dealing with the *social* structures of our time has *got* to be aware of the *personal* sense of isolation and the needs for love and esteem which motivate the people *in* those structures . . . including himself.

While I was wrestling with this dilemma, one of the women, Matey Janata, was talking about women's liberation. But she was saying that men as well as women are feeling trapped and lonely and experiencing acute needs for love, esteem, and self-actualization. What we need is not a church of liberated women, she concluded, but a church of *liberated human beings* who are free to love each other and who can risk their futures to free other people out in the world!

I realized that somehow we in the church have set up a false choice and division—*either* to be prophets *or* lovers. And that neither group really trusts the other. And what God had done for me in those five days was not to give a resolution of the dilemma. But it seemed that he was trying to tell us that he wants us to learn to be both—prophetic and loving—as he has been with us.

Looking back at scenes in the Bible and the church's history, I saw that God has always approached man in his concrete situation with *both* justice and forgiveness, like the "two prongs" of a paradox—one in either hand, as it were. God's presence is always shrouded in paradox on the manward side. He is *always* perfect *righteous judgment* on one hand and yet perfect *mercy* and *love* on the other. And it has been the mysterious discernment of God that has led him to touch his people one time with the finger of righteous confrontation—often just when things appeared to be most prosperous for them—and at other times he has reached out with the hand of mercy and affirmation—just when all seemed lost. And God's criteria concerning which aspect of his nature to reveal apparently centers in the question: "What will bring *ultimate* healing and wholeness to the people?" For God's truth about a social situation often seems to be the opposite of the outward appearance.

But how can we develop a style of living in which we can be prophetic and yet also loving. Most of the so-called prophets I've heard the last few years seemed to have no love at all—for God, for the people, or for themselves—only hate! And then I remembered my experience with our small group, how we had learned that only the person who is beginning to know and *love himself* enough to *confront and affirm his own behavior* can confront and affirm others with real sensitivity.

So before thinking about being "prophetic" we must become liberated enough to discover something of what is inside *us*, or our twisted superegos will distort the gentle voice of discernment, and we may find ourselves beating people with their guilt, coddling them because of ours, or mistaking our own veiled power needs for "the word of God" . . . as so many "prophets" have done.

There are two common traits which seem to be essential for a Christian operating in the structures of the world: The first is God's gift of *discernment,* but since this is a gift, all one can do basically is to prepare a place for it in his life. A small group might provide the conditions for liberation so that the charismatic gift of discernment could be a more effective tool if received.

The second essential trait for a liberated agent of change would seem to be *courage, raw courage.* And that has been the stumbling block for me and for a good many of the people I've talked to about these things: the fear of risking our jobs, reputations, vocational future, etc. And yet I think God actually is going to use those of us who *are* afraid, who *aren't* very stable in our courageousness, who sometimes run like crazy from doing his will, and are afraid to turn loose of our securities!—just as he used men like Moses (see Ex. 4:1–17), Gideon (Judg. 6: 14–40), or Saul (1 Sam. 10:22, 23) in spite of their anxious attempts to avoid God's call to courageous action.

What was it about these men and many others like them which made them usable by God as pivotal voices of change? In every case they finally came to the point at which they could risk turning loose and putting the outcome of their lives in God's hands—even though they were afraid or uncertain.

I realize that some of this line of reasoning about the mixture of fear with courage and the "personal" with the "prophetic" may be specious thinking. But if any of it is true, then there is hope that some of us "lovers" may live as liberated Christian change agents in the structures of the world.

REFERENCES

Bonhoeffer, Dietrich. *The Cost of Discipleship*. New York: The Macmillan Company, 1960 (1st ed. 1949).

Buechner, Frederick. *The Magnificent Defeat*. New York: Seabury Press, 1966.

Cassels, Louis. *The Real Jesus*. New York: Doubleday, 1968.

Clinebell, Howard J., Jr. *Basic Types of Pastoral Counseling*. New York: Abingdon, 1966.

Corsini, Raymond J. *Methods of Group Psychotherapy*. Chicago: William James Press, 1964 (1st ed. 1957).

Frankl, Viktor. *Man's Search for Meaning*. New York: Beacon Press, 1964.

Freud, Sigmund. *A General Introduction to Psychoanalysis*. New York: Washington Square Press, 1960 (1st ed. 1924).

————. *The Standard Edition of the Complete Psychological Works of Sigmund Freud*. Translated and edited by James Strachey. 23 vols. London: Hogarth Press, 1955-66.

Gordon, Thomas. *Group Centered Leadership*. Boston: Houghton Mifflin Company, 1955.

Greeley, Andrew M. *The Jesus Myth*. New York: Doubleday, 1971.

Hall, Calvin S., and Lindzey, Gardner. *Theories of Personality*. New York: John Wiley & Sons, 1957.

Hiltner, Seward. *Pastoral Counseling*. New York: Abingdon, 1949.

Horney, Karen. *American Journal of Psychoanalysis* 48 (1949):9, 3.

Howe, Reuel L. *The Miracle of Dialogue*. Greenwich, Conn.: Seabury Press, 1963.

Jacoby, Jolande. *The Psychology of Carl Jung*. New Haven: Yale University Press, 1962.

James, William. *The Varieties of Religious Experience*. New York: Random House, Modern Library, 1929 (1st ed. 1902).

Jung, C. G. *The Structure and Dynamics of the Psyche*, The Collected Works. Vol. 8. New York: Pantheon Books, 1960, pp. 45-61.

Kempis, Thomas à. *The Imitation of Christ*. London: Collins, 1957.

Kierkegaard, Sören. *Purity of Heart Is to Will One Thing*. New York: Harpers, 1938.

————. *Fear and Trembling*. London: Oxford University Press, 1946.

Kisker, George W. *The Disorganized Personality*. New York: McGraw Hill, 1964.

Knox, John. *Life in Christ Jesus*. New York: Seabury Press, 1966 (1st ed. 1961).

————. *Limits of Unbelief*. New York: Seabury Press, 1970.

Larson, Bruce. *Ask Me to Dance*. Waco, Texas: Word Books, 1972.

Lecky, Prescott. *Self-Consistency: A Theory of Personality*. New York: Island Press, 1945.

Marty, Martin E. *A Short History of Christianity*. New York: World Publishing Co., 1962 (1st ed. 1959).

Maslow, Abraham H. *Motivation and Personality*. New York: Harper & Row, 1970 (1st ed. 1954).

————. *Toward a Psychology of Being*. New York: Van Nostrand Reinhold Company, 1968 (1st ed. 1962).

Mowrer, O. H. "Sin the Lesser of Two Evils." *The American Psychologist* 15 (May 1960): 301.

Oldham, J. H. *Florence Allshorn and the Story of St. Julian's*. New York: Harpers, 1951.

Rogers, Carl H. "Some Observations of the Organization of Personality." *The American Psychologist* 2 (1947): 358-68.

————. *Client Centered Therapy*. Boston: Houghton Mifflin Company, 1965 (1st ed. 1951).

————. *On Encounter Groups*. New York: Harper & Row, 1970.

Rosenbaum, Jean; Shainers, Natalie and Wenkart, Antonio.

Smith, Hannah W. *The Christian's Secret of a Happy Life*. Old Tappan, N. J.: Fleming H. Revell Company, 1968.

Schutz, William C. *Here Comes Everybody*. New York: Harper & Row, 1971.

Stern, Paul J. *The Abnormal Person and His World*. New York: D. Van Nostrand Company, 1964.

Teilhard, Pierre. *Letters from a Traveller*. New York: Harper & Row, Torchbook, 1962 (1st ed. 1956).

————. *The Divine Milieu*. New York: Harper & Row, 1968 (1st ed. 1957).

Temple, William. *Readings in St. John's Gospel*. London: Macmillan, 1963 (1st ed. 1939).

Tillich, Paul. *The Shaking of the Foundations*. London: S. C. M. Press, 1949.

Toffler, Alvin. *Future Shock*. New York: Bantam, 1971.

Tournier, Paul. *The Meaning of Persons.* New York: Harper &
  Row, 1957.
———. *Guilt and Grace.* New York: Harper & Row, 1962.
———. *A Place for You.* New York: Harper & Row, 1968.
Whitehead, Alfred N. *Adventures of Ideas.* New York: Mentor
  Books, 1955 (1st ed. 1933).